SWING
and a
HIT

SWING
and a
HIT

NINE INNINGS OF WHAT BASEBALL TAUGHT ME

PAUL O'NEILL AND JACK CURRY

TWELVE

NEW YORK   BOSTON

Twelve
Hachette Book Group
1290 Avenue of the Americas, New York, NY 10104
twelvebooks.com
twitter.com/twelvebooks

First Edition: May 2022

Twelve is an imprint of Grand Central Publishing. The Twelve name and logo are trademarks of Hachette Book Group, Inc.

The publisher is not responsible for websites (or their content) that are not owned by the publisher.

The Hachette Speakers Bureau provides a wide range of authors for speaking events. To find out more, go to www.hachettespeakersbureau.com or call (866) 376-6591.

Library of Congress Control Number: 2021952466

ISBNs: 9781538709610 (hardcover), 9781538709634 (ebook)

Printed in the United States of America

LSC-C

Printing 1, 2022

To my family, my friends, and the fans. Thanks for everything.
—Paul O'Neill

For Rob, a devoted big brother who taught me how to throw a ball and swing a bat and cultivated my lifelong love of baseball. Thanks for always being there.

For Mrs. O, a loving mother-in-law whose abundant baseball knowledge was surpassed only by her endless wisdom and guidance. We all miss you.
—Jack Curry

CONTENTS

SWING
and a
HIT

———◦◦———

CHAPTER 1

Breaking into the Majors with Pete Rose, the Hit King

I kept peeking to my left and right in the dugout, almost waiting for a security guard to forcefully grab my arm and tell me it was time to leave. I was wearing a splashy Cincinnati Reds uniform with the number 21 and sitting with the other players, because I was finally one of them. I was part of the team I adored while growing up in Columbus, Ohio, so I was exactly where I always wanted to be. But I felt like an impostor. Did I really belong?

I was eight days into my major-league career, a long-awaited journey that fortunately started with me notching a hit in my first plate appearance. Obviously, that was a monumental relief. But, with such a flimsy big-league résumé, I was still uncertain and I was still hundreds of at bats away from feeling secure.

Everywhere I turned, I saw another famous face that floored me because these were the men I had idolized. I was playing beside the incomparable Pete Rose, the clutch Tony Pérez, and the reliable Davey Concepción, the players from the vaunted Big Red Machine championship teams I had imitated while imagining Game 7s in my backyard. Those guys were my heroes while they were winning World Series titles in 1975 and 1976. Sitting in that Reds dugout, trying to prevent my knees from shaking and my eyes from growing as wide as Frisbees, I still felt like that kid hitting tennis balls with a 28-ounce Louisville Slugger, not an authentic major leaguer. It was so surreal.

I had endless baseball dreams, gigantic baseball dreams—just like thousands and thousands of other kids in Ohio. My dad, Charles "Chick" O'Neill, was a former minor league pitcher, and he taught me to work harder than everyone else and hit line drives. As he watched me stand tall and whip my bat through the strike zone from the left side, he also told me my swing reminded him of Ted Williams's. Ted Williams? Even as a six-year-old kid, that was a magical name for me to hear. I can still hear him saying that, the kind of unforgettable compliment that a proud father would make and the kind of compliment that I hung on to like a life preserver and used as motivation throughout my career.

My father's influence was with me for every at bat of my seventeen-year major league career because he was the first prominent and knowledgeable voice I absorbed regarding the art of hitting. For all 2,190 of my hits (including the regular season and postseason), my dad had an impact. He would throw endless rounds of batting practice, he would preach about hitting liners, and he would teach me, coach me, and never lambaste me. After the most depressing of childhood losses in which I went 0 for 4 or made an error and wanted to hide behind a tree, my father's hopeful attitude always made me excited to jump into the Ford Ranchero with him and get ready for the next ice-cream cone and the next baseball adventure.

From an excitable and energetic boy aggressively swinging a bat, I morphed into a much more emotional hitter, who was stubborn and studious and who had a serious approach to hitting a baseball. My best and most comfortable approach was to swing so that I connected with the top half of the baseball, not the lower half, and not trying to swing under the baseball. As my swing stayed on top of the ball, my bat would level out through the strike zone and I would end up hitting a lot of line drives. At the end of my swing, I would elevate my bat and have a slight uppercut. But I always started my swing on a level plane because that kept my bat in the strike zone longer. Unless I hit a baseball powerfully and squarely, my line drives didn't typically leave the ballpark. But line drives do find the outfield grass, and they do find the outfield gaps, and that's what I was trying to do as a hitter.

These days, there's a legion of prominent and talented hitters who have massive uppercut swings because they want to swing under the baseball to get the ball in the air and blast it over the fence. They are chasing home runs, and I can't blame them for doing that because they're chasing the biggest and most lucrative prize in the sport. Teams dig the long ball, and home runs are being clubbed in historic numbers. There were 6,776 homers hit in the majors in 2019, an all-time record that obliterated the previous one from 2017 by 11 percent.

The term launch angle, which measures the vertical angle at which a baseball leaves a bat after a player makes contact, didn't exist when I was playing. Neither did exit velocity, which measures the speed (in miles per hour) at which a baseball travels off the bat. Generally speaking, the harder a baseball is hit, the more likely it is to rocket past or around a fielder or over a fence and turn into a base hit. Nowadays, Little Leaguers know the definition of those terms and try to be just like the idols they watch on television. In the Yankees dugout, teammates watch Giancarlo Stanton—the king of exit velocity—scorch another ball and they ask, "Did he hit that one 120?" Of course, that means 120 miles per hour.

There are so many different ways to be a successful hitter because hitting is about feeling comfortable and confident and making sure every aspect of your swing is in sync. From the way you stride forward to the way you rotate your hips to the way you power your bat toward the baseball, every action has to blend seamlessly. That comfort and that confidence will be different for each hitter. While I was never a proponent of criticizing the way any hitter hits or forcing my ideas on any hitter, I will explain why my style worked for me, why I think my style has staying power, and why I think my style can work for others.

As hitters graduate to the highest levels of the sport, they are going to hear different voices flooding their brains with opinions about hitting. Tons of voices. Every day of my professional career, I had conversations about hitting with teammates, coaches, and former players. Some of these conversations were great and helpful. Some of these conversations were trivial and useless. What I learned is that hitters need to determine what is right for them and stay loyal to what makes them comfortable and successful. But that attitude didn't mean that I was resistant to making changes.

Rick Down, the Yankees' hitting coach, helped me implement a leg kick when I was traded to New York, and that timing mechanism was crucial to my balance in the box and bolstered my career. I hit .259 with a .336 on-base percentage, a .431 slugging percentage and 96 homers in 799 games in Cincinnati, and I hit .303 with a .377 OBP, a .492 slugging percentage and 185 homers in 1,254 games in New York. With the new leg kick and the new way of hitting, I was a much better hitter with the Yankees.

My strategy was to listen to what coaches and teammates offered, determine if it fit into the way I wanted to hit and if it produced positive results, and then make any potential alterations. I was open to tweaks, but wouldn't change just because a coach or a manager insisted his idea was a good one. I believe hitters need to be dedicated to who they are and how they are comfortable hitting. Pete Rose told me that all the time. So did Ted Williams when I had a memorable phone conversation with him. Those legends simply validated what I had always felt about hitting. (By the way, I will discuss that chat with Williams later in the book.)

Once my dad taught me to hit line drives and explained the wisdom of using the whole field, I was forever a disciple of that hitting approach. That became my style and that remained the style I was comfortable using. Because I was six feet four and 210 pounds, there were some people, including my manager

Lou Piniella, who believed I should be more of a home-run hitter. But I really wasn't a true home-run hitter. Didn't you see me argue with Kramer about homers in that *Seinfeld* episode?

For me to hit a homer, my swing would have to start early to be out in front of the pitch and then I would need to make perfect and powerful contact and, most likely, pull the ball. That's not who I was. I watch in awe as Aaron Judge uses his uppercut swing and bashes 450-foot homers. That's who he is. Judge has stressed the importance of remaining anchored on his back hip because, if his lower body is under control, his head will remain still as he unleashes his swing. When Judge does that and executes his swing properly, he said it allows his bat path to get in the strike zone earlier and stay in the zone longer. That gives him a better chance to stay through pitches consistently and drive the ball to right routinely. Judge has described his bat path as being more like a Ferris wheel than a merry-go-round, meaning that his upper body and his swing tilt like a Ferris wheel and allow him to be quick to the ball and to elevate the ball. Sometimes, he won't generate his best swing but is still able to produce enough power to hit a homer. I didn't hit majestic shots like the very talented and very powerful Judge. I hit line drives—by choice. I wanted to put the ball in play.

Striking out was embarrassing to me, something that has changed in today's game because it's widely accepted for power hitters to whiff more than 200 times a year. In my career, I only exceeded 100 strikeouts three times, and my highest strikeout total was 107, a number that still irritates me. That's too many empty at bats. Avoiding strikeouts and making contact requires making adjustments with two strikes, which doesn't happen as often today. I see so many players still take their home-run swing with two strikes, which is one reason we see so many strikeouts. Obviously, the proliferation of flamethrowers—each team seemingly has about a half dozen pitchers who throw one hundred miles per hour—has a lot to do with all the strikeouts, too. But, especially as a young player, I always felt my job was to put the ball in play and to put pressure on the defense. I despised strikeouts and still do.

I will jump off my soapbox about the value of hitting line drives to concede there was one at bat, one amazingly important at bat, in which I wish one of my liners had soared a little higher. When the Yankees were down to our final out against Cleveland in Game 5 of the 1997 American League Division Series, I blasted a liner off of José Mesa, a pitcher I handled well with 9 hits in 11 at bats in my career, which includes the postseason. The ball rocketed to right field and I was pleading for it to leave the ballpark and tie the game. "Get higher," I begged. "Get higher." But it didn't. The liner smacked about halfway up the fence. Another six feet higher, about the length of two baseball bats, and it would have been a game-tying homer. Because I hit the ball so hard, the right fielder retrieved it quickly and I had to hustle, scramble, and slide awkwardly on my right side to get into second and secure a double. That desperation dive into second earned me the nickname "the Warrior" from George Steinbrenner, the Yankees' principal owner.

Anyway, after my near miss, Mesa retired Bernie Williams and our season ended. If only my line drive swing had produced more of a fly ball in that spot, we might have won that game. I thought about that at bat for a few months, my off-season clouded by our lost opportunity to defend our 1996 title. The pain stayed, as did my affinity for hitting line drives.

It would have been so rewarding and so memorable to hit that ball slightly higher off Mesa and tie the game with a homer. But, as much as I've pondered that possibility and longed for that outcome over the years, I did everything I wanted to do in that at bat. I waited for a good pitch to hit and I ripped that ball on a line drive to right field. That's who I was and that's who I always wanted to be. Sometimes, the line drive falls short or doesn't fall in at all. But that at bat is the type of at bat I aspired to have during my career, especially after I fought through my early self-doubts.

Back in 1985 with the Reds, I was still trying to prove myself, like I always did as the youngest child chasing around my four older brothers and one older sister. Those early major-league moments were thrilling, but no matter how successful I had been in the minor leagues, I couldn't always suppress my doubts. Doubts about my swing, doubts about my abilities, doubts about whether I could hit against the best pitchers in the world. I gradually became more confident because I had a .285 average in more than 2,200 plate appearances in the minors and had continued to learn about my strengths as a hitter, but there's nothing that matches the jump from Triple-A to the majors. Nothing is even close, because the pitchers are smarter, better, and more creative. I felt hopeful with each advancement from Single-A to Double-A to Triple-A. However, when I sauntered into a major-league clubhouse for the first time, I was numb and jittery. That promotion was everything I had worked to achieve since I was a five-year-old, but I didn't walk in with swagger in my step. I tiptoed into the room like an extra who had a twenty-second scene in a two-hour movie.

As those doubts swirled inside my head, I felt more like a fan than an actual player on September 11, 1985. It was one of the most anticipated days in Cincinnati sports history, because Rose needed one more hit to break Ty Cobb's all-time hit record. On the previous night, he had gone 0 for 4. Reds fans were restless and growing more restless. I loved Pete Rose. I loved the way he hustled around the field, I loved his bravado, and I loved the way he willed himself to smack all those hits. Pretty much everyone in Cincinnati loved Pete, too, because he was a son of the city, a hometown grinder who was about to become the Hit King.

Pete was our player-manager, so he was my boss and my teammate, but I had had only a few brief conversations with him during spring training. At that moment, he was more of a poster on the bedroom wall to me than someone I knew intimately. I didn't initiate much conversation with the players I considered my heroes because I was worried about saying too much or saying the wrong thing. Many times, silence was the best plan. If I had spoken extensively with Pete at that time, I would have told the switch-hitter how beautifully I mimicked his hunched over batting stance from the left side when I goofed around with my siblings.

That day was a blur of excitement for me, with everyone scrambling to get tickets to the game and television stations covering Rose's pursuit with intensity usually reserved for an election night. I watched forty-four-year-old Pete closely, and he was his spirited self, fielding grounders at first base before taking some familiar swings in batting practice. He also spoke to the news media for about thirty minutes, something he did every day as the history-pursuing player-manager, and something that would have been unsettling for me.

When I was pummeling the baseball and batting .405 with the Yankees in mid-June of 1994, the questions about my quest for the elusive .400 plateau, which was last achieved by Williams in 1941, intensified. I didn't enjoy the attention. Sometimes I would scowl as I sat by my locker, rest my forearms on my thighs, lean forward, and try to look unapproachable. I understood the reporters had a job to do and I respected that. Heck, my sister Molly was a reporter for *The New York Times*! But I never liked getting too in-depth before games, even telling some reporters, "Nothing I say to you is going to help me get a hit tonight."

But talking about hitting never bothered Pete. He relished it. He was a hitter who enjoyed joking and sparring with anyone, a prolific singles hitter who always seemed prepared with a snappy response or a clever one-liner. Anyway, there were 47,237 pairs of eyes on Rose as he strolled to the plate in the first inning at Riverfront Stadium. I always admired how Pete looked extremely confident as a hitter—a hitter who dictated the at bat and who even looked cool as he took pitches. He would twist his neck toward the catcher and stare the baseball into the catcher's glove, like an investigator looking for forensic evidence.

Eric Show, a workhorse right-hander who won 12 games and pitched 233 innings that season, was on the mound for the San Diego Padres. Pete took Show's first pitch for a ball that was off the plate, then he fouled off a fastball, and backed away as the third pitch sailed inside. After each pitch, Pete stepped out of the batter's box, spread the dirt with his cleats, or grabbed the handle of his black bat to get more pine tar on his batting gloves. Then, as flashbulbs popped and the fans chanted his name, Rose smacked a 2-1 slider into left-center field for a clean single. It was the record-breaking 4,192nd hit of his career, and fittingly, it was a typical Rose hit. Pete rounded first, clapped his hands, and the fans exploded. I stood in the first-base dugout, absolutely speechless.

All of a sudden, everyone emptied out of the dugout and dashed onto the field to swarm Pete. I didn't know Pete nearly as well as my teammates did, but I was savvy enough to follow them and to be more than a mannequin. As everyone embraced Pete, I wasn't sure what to do. Mostly, I just hovered around the edges of the crowd, acting like I belonged. I was fortunate enough to subsequently play on five World Series champions and play in three perfect games during my career, but that record-breaking moment will always be one of my top 10 baseball experiences. I had nothing to do with it, but it was so rewarding to witness history.

Just as I had maneuvered myself around the tangle of white-and-red uniformed bodies to possibly shake Pete's hand, Pérez and Concepción lifted him over their shoulders and everyone screeched with delight. Marge Schott, the Reds' owner, shuffled onto the field to hug Pete, and a gorgeous red Corvette

11

with the license plate PR-4192 was driven through an outfield gate and delivered to Rose. Eventually, Pete Jr., Rose's fifteen-year-old son, came onto the field in a Reds uniform with ROSE and 14 on the back and embraced his dad. For a few minutes, Pete stood near first base all by himself, the fireworks hailing, the confetti flying, and the cheering escalating.

"It was the only time in my life that I was on a baseball field," Rose said, "and I didn't know what the hell to do."

I saw Pete stare up at the dark sky and wipe away a tear with his batting glove, and I figured he was paying homage to his father, which he acknowledged after the game. After seven minutes of endless adulation, during which a stone-faced Show sat on the mound for a while and waited, the game continued. And, in the biggest of footnotes, we won, 2-0. Pete, who also tripled for his 4,193rd hit, scored both runs. It wasn't shocking for me to later find out that he turned to Schott during the celebration and said, "Let's play ball. I want to score this run." President Ronald Reagan called and congratulated Pete after the game, and in Pete's true, sassy way, he told the most powerful man in the free world that he had missed seeing a good game.

Eight days earlier, Pete was actually congratulating me. Obviously, it wasn't for a historic hit, but for being a September call-up to the Reds after hitting .305 with 7 homers and 74 runs batted in for the Triple-A Denver Zephyrs. When Pete spoke to me in the visiting manager's office in St. Louis, he was sitting behind a desk and he was both casual and blunt. He stressed that the Reds were still clinging to their pennant hopes, as we were nine and a half games behind the first-place Los Angeles Dodgers, so I shouldn't expect to play much. He told me to relax, watch what was happening, and learn through osmosis. Pete's words calmed me because they allowed me to exhale and not instantly obsess about trying to hit major league pitchers.

But, of course, I watched Rose's best-laid plans for me evaporate. On my first day as a Red, our game with the Cardinals at Busch Stadium included several pitching changes, and a pinch-hitting opportunity arose in the eighth inning.

"Grab a bat, kid!" Rose shouted.

Me? Wasn't I supposed to just sit here and learn? I became very uneasy. I was nervous putting on my uniform for the first time and I was nervous taking batting practice for the first time. Now multiply that by about a thousand as I readied to face Jeff Lahti, a right-hander who threw hard sliders and harder fastballs, and who had pitched for the 1982 World Series champion Cardinals. It's a cliché, but my heart was beating through my chest as I picked up a bat and officially became a major leaguer.

Everything happened so fast. I don't remember walking to the plate or digging into the box. In the blink of an eye, I swung at a first-pitch fastball and lined a shot to right-center field. I was fortunate that Lahti threw me a fastball. As a very anxious hitter, I probably would have swung at a curveball that bounced five feet in front of the plate. It was just a quick, reflexive action to see a fastball for the first pitch I had ever seen in the majors and to connect with it for a hit. Honestly, it was a relief. An utter relief.

My legs felt wobbly as I ran to first base, almost as if I were dragging them along with the rest of my body. Because my legs felt like Jell-O for those few seconds, I didn't even try to sprint for second. I think I turned a double into a single, but I was OK with that. I had my first hit. I wasn't about to ruin the moment by running into an out at second.

We lost the game, but my mission was to rush back to the hotel so I could call my parents and tell them all the details about my first hit. These days, a player could simply use his cell phone to call from the clubhouse or the team bus, but I had to wait to use the hotel phone and the wait was excruciating. I wanted to shout or scream or maybe even cry, but that wouldn't have looked cool around my teammates. Impatiently, I waited.

Finally, about ninety minutes after the game had ended, I burst into my hotel room, punched numbers into the phone, and called home. My father answered. I was just about to tell him everything that happened and tell him how I hit a line drive the way that he had always taught me, when he said, "We saw it! Congratulations." I didn't realize the game had been televised, so my mother and father saw my single, saw me stop at first base and try not to crack a smile, and even heard Joe Morgan, the Hall-of-Fame second baseman and television analyst, comment on my first hit. It was as joyful and as relieved as I'd ever felt on a baseball field.

Interestingly, Lahti later said he understood the feeling of being anchored on first base after a hit: "He worked his butt off his whole life to get where he wanted and then you want to run and you can't," Lahti said. "My first base hit came against the Mets in New York. I pulled a sharp shot down the line that hit off the wall, except I ended up with a single because I stood at home plate and thought, 'I hit it.'"

After my call-up in 1985, I still spent more time at Triple A in 1986 before hitting .256 with a .488 slugging percentage in 84 games with the Reds in 1987 and feeling like I belonged in the majors. But even as I made progress and was told I would be a central part of the Reds' future, I still had doubts I would ever be good enough to be a competent big-league hitter. Many nights, I put my head on the pillow and reviewed at bats.

Whenever I struggled in the minors, it was a reminder that hitting .500 in high school is dramatically different than playing professionally. In an instant, I had a high school diploma on the wall and a $35,000 signing bonus from the Reds (and the powder blue Firebird I bought with the money), and I was surrounded by players who were as good or better than me. I studied all those players, watching their swings and their approaches, and because it's human nature, evaluating myself against them. Am I as good as Player X or Player Y?

The minor leagues were challenging because the competition was way better than what I was accustomed to, because I wasn't used to being away from home for that long, and because of the sheer number of games that I was playing. I played about 20 games a year in high school in the chilly climate of Ohio. Then I got drafted in the third round, and I was playing in more than 60 games in my first year in Rookie League ball, then close to 140 games a year after that. Even if my statistics ended up being acceptable to me, there were so many ups and downs along the way to get to that .300 average.

I knew how to focus on baseball. But on some of those long bus trips, I did wonder about the family barbecues and birthday parties I was missing back home. Still, as much as I had some dreary and doubting periods, I never lost sight of the ultimate goal of playing in the majors. That was my obsession.

Rose had an obsession with hitting, which meshed nicely with my personality. Like Pete, I thought about hitting all day long. As improbable as it seems, I believed I could and should get a hit in every plate appearance. That's insane. But it's the way I felt, and that competitive desire drove me. Of course, I knew Pete was the same way, and that's why I enjoyed talking with him and learning from him.

Pete worked with me on the mental side of the game by keeping things simple and telling me I needed to stay out of my own way. By that, he meant that I had a tendency to over-think things, and at that time, he was right. I always treated every at bat intensely, but as I was trying to claw my way into the majors, I was even more desperate. Baseball was supposed to be my livelihood. I didn't have much of a backup plan.

If I had a good game with a couple of hits, Pete would constantly remind me to maintain that positive feeling and that belief in myself. Pete was a career .303 hitter who was fanatical about hitting above .300, which he did in fifteen different seasons, so he spoke my language. I know that baseball perspectives have been modified, and I know that on-base percentage is considered a better way to evaluate a hitter's contributions because it recognizes all of a batter's plate appearances. That's logical, and that's what Gene "Stick" Michael, the Yankees' general manager who had traded for me, used to espouse. He would stare at a stat sheet and circle the number of hits *and* walks that a player had. But I broke into the majors at a time when having solid at bats, putting the ball in play, and yes, hitting .300, were my goals. Today, many hitters would rather go 1 for 4 with a homer than go 3 for 4 with 3 singles and 1 RBI. I would still take the 3 singles.

And, if I were compiling a lineup, I would still prefer a balanced one that has a mixture of contact hitters and power hitters, like the lineups we had with the late '90s Yankees. I've never been a supporter of all-or-nothing lineups that feature all power hitters, because I think pitchers can get comfortable against the same type of hitters and can collect lots of swings and misses.

Anyway, as for Pete's advice, his words may have sounded simple, but those words resonated with me because they came from an outstanding hitter.

"Listen, here's my philosophy on hitting," Rose said. "Everyone who is a hitter has an expertise. Just go out and do the things you do well and do them on a consistent basis. If you can't run, don't try to steal bases. If you can't hit home runs, don't try to swing from your ass. Everybody has something they can do."

More than anything, Pete understood me as a hitter.

"Paul had a big swing," Rose said. "He had great eyes. He didn't strike out a lot and that's unusual for a big guy with a big swing. At an early age, Paul understood how important the whole field was. That's why they have the whole field out there. Use it."

"Today, they put shifts on all these guys," Rose added.

"There's no chance of hitting .300. If they shift you today, there ain't no way you can hit .300. Paul hit the ball everywhere. He wasn't just a pull hitter. He hit the ball to left and to center. He was strong enough to hit home runs, but he wasn't really a home run hitter. He was just a really good hitter."

As I evolved as a hitter, I learned that my best approach was to look for a pitch that was out over the plate and to stay out there. I wanted the ball to be in the middle of the plate or on the outside part of the plate. I didn't want to look inside. Eventually, I felt that if I did everything I was supposed to do in looking for a pitch that was middle or away, I could adjust to anything that the pitcher did.

There are so many smart theories about hitting, but this is the approach that worked for me: hitting on top of the ball, trying to hit the ball the other way, and controlling the at bat. I played with many great hitters, like Don Mattingly and Jorge Posada, and they would often guess fastball or breaking pitch when they were at the plate. Donnie was a very smart hitter who studied pitchers and who could outwit pitchers. As a catcher whose livelihood was to scrutinize other batters, Jorge felt that he knew the way teams would try to get him out. I had deep respect for both of them and understood why they guessed. But I didn't like to guess on pitches because I felt that was allowing the pitcher to dictate what might happen in the at bat, and my guess was contingent on what he was doing. I wanted to control what I did. Even when I decided where to station myself in the batter's box, I always stood at the back of the box. Some teammates suggested I inch up in the box to negate a pitcher's breaking ball, but again, I felt like that was adjusting to the pitcher. And if I adjusted to the pitcher, that meant he was already cluttering my mind and I had put myself in an inferior position.

Joe Torre, my intelligent and always soothing manager on the Yankees, validated my approach about looking for pitches that were middle and away when he told me, "If a pitcher is going to throw you on the inside corner, how many of them are going to be good enough to hit that spot three straight times?" Exactly! Joe, who hit .297 with over 2,300 hits in his career, preached what I was already thinking. Most pitchers will never be as precise as a control artist like Greg Maddux. They routinely miss locations with their pitches. I didn't want to guess and look for a certain pitch that I really didn't want to hit. I looked for the pitch I preferred because that played to my strengths. My hope was I would put myself in the same hitting position every time so that I could hit the pitch I desired or acclimate to every other pitch. If I got the pitch that was middle or middle away, I could drive it to left-center field or hit it up the middle, or if I was fooled, I might end up pulling it to right field. If I was behind it, I could even use an inside-out swing to hit it to left field. But that approach gave me the chance to hit every pitch.

In addition, if I was looking for a pitch that was inside, I would have a tendency to start my swing too soon and allow my body to fly open and unleash a weaker swing. As soon as I opened up to anticipate that inside pitch, I would lose any chance to squarely hit a pitch that was on the outside. So, by doing that, I would have lost the pitch I really wanted to hit because I was trying to protect against him coming inside.

Again, how many pitchers can throw three straight perfect pitches inside to beat me? Still, it was a mental tug-of-war at the plate to not be worried about that inside pitch. If they busted me inside for a strike or if I fouled a tough pitch off, I would usually step out of the box, eliminate that pitch from my mind, and focus on what I was trying to do as a hitter, not what he was trying to do as a pitcher. That was the competitor in me, making sure I did it my way.

"He was one of the most competitive guys I ever managed," Rose said. "He hated to lose to the point where it bothered him."

Pete was right. Anyone who ever saw me argue with an umpire, fling a bat, or smash a water cooler knows Pete was right. Pete offered me a lot of wisdom, including passionately telling me that Ted Kluszewski was the best hitting coach the Reds ever had. That's a statement that should be painted on billboards in Cincinnati. Big Klu was the Reds' hitting coach for nine seasons, including for the title teams in 1975 and 1976, and then became a minor league hitting instructor in 1979.

On an overcast morning in Tampa, Florida, in October 1982, I was a nineteen-year-old who had just finished a 116-game season for the Single A Cedar Rapids Reds. And now it was time for more baseball lessons in the Instructional League. I was getting a chance to follow my dreams, but in those initial days, the dream felt like it was a thousand miles away. I knew I would need a lot of help to achieve my dreams. And then I met Ted, this incredible soothsayer of a hitting instructor. That was one of the most fortuitous meetings of my life.

Given that I was an anxious kid who was searching for

guidance and reassurance, Ted was the perfect coach. He was a mountain of a man at six feet two and 240 pounds, and a man whose robust biceps and mighty swings were his calling card during his career. Ted's biceps were so huge that he cut the sleeves off his jersey because he didn't want the fabric to inhibit the movement of his arms and shoulders as he swung. The Reds weren't pleased with his tailoring, but they eventually made everyone wear sleeveless uniforms.

During Ted's fifteen-year career, he hit .300 on seven different occasions and hit 40 or more homers in three straight seasons. But here's what made Ted such a distinctive hitter: he combined tremendous power with the ability to put the ball in play. Ted could clobber homers without producing the endless swings and misses that have become so prevalent and so accepted in today's game.

"I didn't just hate to strike out," Ted told me. "I hated the thought of striking out."

Check out these eye-popping numbers. In 1953, Ted hit 40 homers and whiffed 34 times. In 1954, he blasted 49 homers and struck out 35 times. And in 1955, Ted smashed 47 homers and struck out 40 times! These days, some of baseball's prolific power hitters might strike out 40 times in one month. Since Ted last accomplished that feat in 1955, no 40-homer hitter has ever whiffed as few as 40 times. Yes, I wanted to learn from this man.

As imposing as Ted was, he spoke the language of hitting simply and reassuringly, similar to the way my father taught me. From my first moments in the batting cage, I recall Ted standing behind me, watching every swing and commenting on almost every swing. He was often positive, but he was always honest. And that's what I needed. I needed someone I trusted to tell me the truth about my last swing, and if it wasn't an effective swing, I needed him to explain what I should do better. Ted was that man. Ted was my swing whisperer, analyzing everything I did and telling me how to do it better.

Since I was a left-handed hitter who was adept at hitting line drives and making contact, Ted explained the importance of having me stay on the outside pitch to hit it left-center or left field. That approach became my bread-and-butter during my career and it was honed with Ted. If I didn't stay on the baseball, Ted would sigh and say, "Oh, you left me."

Those words forever rang in my ears. That meant I had been too quick or too eager and I hadn't kept my swing on a path to stay with the pitch. In the beginning, as Ted kept saying, "Oh, you left me," I'm not sure I understood the gravity of what he was saying. I was just trying to hit a liner to left. But, as we worked on a daily basis in the Instructional League, his words became a mantra for me, a golden rule.

I could hear him saying, "Oh, you left me," and that was a constant reminder of what I didn't want to do. I didn't want my swing to leave me. I wanted my swing to stay on the ball and make solid contact. The days of facing 75-mile-per-hour fastballs in high school were long gone, and Ted was preparing me for what lay ahead. To this day, I'm amazed at how quickly he assessed what type of hitter I was and provided me with some simple yet powerful hitting advice. "Oh, you left me," is something I heard in my head for the next couple of decades.

"Ted couldn't make it as a hitting coach today," Rose said

sarcastically. "The one thing he never did to young players? He never confused them. He never made them confused in the batter's box. I had the right guy in Ted Kluszewski to teach our young hitters. And he loved Paul."

The feeling was mutual. I loved interacting with Ted, especially as I advanced through the minor-league system and became a regular in Cincinnati. I was Ted's pupil, and I could tell how proud he was that I became a contributor in the big leagues and stayed loyal to the hitter I was and the hitter he had helped me become. After Ted died of a heart attack in 1988, I was distraught. I sorely miss our conversations, which were always warm and almost always about hitting.

While I've never considered myself a serious memorabilia collector, Eleanor, Ted's wife, stunned me after his death by giving me a weathered baseball from his collection. The artifact has Babe Ruth's signature on one side and Hank Aaron's on the other. Ruth was the home-run king with 714 homers, until Aaron surpassed him in 1974. Aaron, who was so kind and was such a gentleman when I had the opportunity to speak with him, blasted 755 career homers, which Barry Bonds eclipsed in 2007. Bonds finished with 762. That signed baseball is so meaningful to me because of those two iconic Hall-of-Fame players, but even more so because it reminds me of Ted. I've never asked anyone what the baseball is worth. I already know how priceless it is to me.

Voices. Baseball players will hear lots of voices, well-meaning voices filled with tips and suggestions and advice. As I mentioned earlier, it's important for a player to be selective and stubborn, at times, and listen to the voices that make him feel the most comfortable and the most confident.

My father, Pete Rose, and Ted Kluszewski all gave me wonderful, timeless hitting advice, words of wisdom that made me better. But, as my career blossomed in Cincinnati, I would soon have to say goodbye to Rose. All of baseball would have to do the same. And then I would encounter a feisty, strong-willed, and smart hitting voice whose views clashed with my thoughts on hitting. The road to being a successful hitter is long and winding and includes many obstacles. I respected Lou Piniella, my new manager with the Reds, but my road to hitting success, based on my definition of it, was about to get more complicated.

CHAPTER 2

Taking Swings with Sweet Lou

Opening Day. Mention those two words and there's no need to say anything else. I've always thought those words were two of the most magical words in sports. We all know what Opening Day is and what it signifies. It's about a new season and a rebirth. And every baseball player hopes it's the start of an unforgettable journey that will end with a championship.

When I was playing for the Julian Speer A's in Little League, or with Brookhaven High School in Columbus, I was so excited for our first game—our own version of Opening Day—that I would try my uniform on before I went to sleep. Then I would place it neatly on my bed to have it ready to wear as soon as I woke up. If I could have slept in it, I would have done that, too. That's how meaningful the first day of baseball was to me. That enthusiastic boy was still a big part of me as I rushed to Riverfront Stadium to play for the Cincinnati Reds on April 3, 1989.

But this season opener was different, and it was impossible

not to notice and feel that. Pete Rose, our iconic manager, was being investigated by Major League Baseball for what was believed to be illegal gambling activities. When Pete marched onto the field before the game, he was engulfed by reporters. This wasn't that unusual, because it was Opening Day and he was our talkative manager. But because of the gambling questions hovering over Pete, this was a different kind of interview session.

One reporter asked Pete if he had bet on baseball games, and Pete said, "No comment." Then Pete said he would end the interview if the reporter asked any more questions about it. The reporter stopped, but that kind of exchange was the way the rest of the season would unfold for Rose. Questions about on-the-field baseball topics became secondary in many of his interviews.

Not surprisingly, the fans continued to adore Pete, and he received a pair of standing ovations before the first pitch had been thrown. Yes, even with the allegations about Pete's possible misdeeds swirling around, Cincinnati loved him. There were 55,385 fans at Riverfront, and every single one of them stood and cheered for their local hero. Standing on the field, seeing and hearing the fans express their affection for Rose, it was evident that this group still considered him a deity.

I had butterflies in my stomach before the game, because I was always nervous before season openers. Who isn't? When teammates told me that my jersey had my name spelled as O'NEIL and was missing one L, I thought they were teasing me with a belated April Fools' Day joke. As more players told me the same thing, I looked in the mirror and realized the tailor who prepared the uniform had forgotten an *L*. Oh well, there was nothing that could be done about it now.

We were playing the World Series champion Los Angeles Dodgers, and they were much more concerning to me than my misspelled name. In my first at bat, my anxiety percolating, I managed to walk against Tim Belcher. Or did I? As I jogged to first, Eddie Murray, the Dodgers' first baseman, looked at me like I was crazy. I wasn't crazy, but my math was off. The count was only 3-2. I sheepishly returned to the plate. Thankfully, I drilled the next pitch for a double.

A misspelled name on my jersey? A walk that wasn't a walk? What other bizarre things were going to happen in this season opener? Fortunately, there were no other odd moments or weird occurrences. Instead, it ended up being a fantastic day as I clubbed a three-run homer and went 4 for 4 as we stopped the Dodgers, 6-4. On a day when so much of the pre-game attention was on Rose, I was happy to contribute to an eventful win.

"He had a better opening day," said Rose, "than I ever put together in my career."

Pete's awkward situation lingered over the team and created a lot more commotion and media attention than the Reds would have normally received. The questions about betting were serious, causing everyone in the baseball world to wonder what could happen to Rose.

I must stress this: Pete was excellent at not letting anything distract him. The world could be crumbling around him (and as we eventually learned, it was), but once Pete put on his uniform and devised our lineup, his focus was on baseball. He used to always say that he was born and bred to play baseball, and in this instance, he was born and bred to be our manager. Even as that job was getting closer to being taken away from him.

As a player, I always respected and tried to trust my manager. For the longest time, that's the attitude I had about Pete and his situation. As mammoth a story as it became, and as much as it occupied Rose's energy, it wasn't something that permeated my world on a 24-7 basis. Since I didn't have the lengthy relationship with Pete that other players and members of the organization had, I was on the outskirts of the story. Reporters didn't ask me many questions about Pete that season. It wouldn't have mattered if they did, because I didn't know anything, plain and simple. I felt sympathy for Pete and what he was experiencing, but I was so far removed from that situation that I didn't have any information to provide.

In addition, my policy was to never say anything negative or critical about my manager. The manager was our leader, and he was my boss, and I wasn't going to say anything that might end up angering him. Naturally, in this delicate situation involving Pete, I stayed mum. Most of the time, I learned details about Rose's situation when I read about it in the morning newspaper. Quite often, there would be an article about our game flanked by an article about Pete's ongoing saga. And actually, it was fine with me to get the updates that way. I've never been a clubhouse lawyer or a clubhouse gossiper. I was simply trying to help Rose and the Reds by being the most productive player I could be.

It might seem callous to say this, but the players weren't obsessing about Pete's status. We were thinking about winning games. Once a player takes the field, he has a job to do. For those three hours, we needed to perform at a high level and try to win. We were tied for first place in early June, but we couldn't sustain it. We had too many injuries and too much inconsistent play. I was leading the team with 62 runs batted in when I fractured my left thumb diving for a ball in late July. I missed about six weeks.

As we navigated through our soap opera of a season, Pete's fate was finally announced on August 24. Baseball Commissioner A. Bartlett Giamatti held a press conference in New York and said Rose had been permanently banned from baseball. The five-page agreement signed by Giamatti and Rose didn't specifically state that Rose had bet on games. But, in a subsequent response to a reporter's question, Giamatti said that, based on the evidence gathered, he believed Rose had bet on baseball and had bet on the Reds.

On that same day, Pete held a press conference at Riverfront Stadium. It was an ominous and depressing scene for the fans who had always loved him and for the players who had respected him, too. Wiping away tears at one point, Pete said he didn't bet on baseball. After years passed, he did admit to it. And we all know that's something players, coaches, and managers are strictly forbidden from doing. "I've made some mistakes," Rose said that day, "and I'm being punished for them."

Oddly enough, I was signing autographs at a card show in Lexington, Kentucky, on the day Rose's permanent suspension was announced. When a reporter asked for my reaction to the news, I described it as a sad day for Pete and said the Reds players were all sad for him. I knew how much baseball meant to Pete, and I knew how much it pained him to have that connection stripped away. The reporter asked if I thought the decision was fair, and I repeated what Rose had said about it being a fair punishment. I floated the idea of him apply-ing for reinstatement and returning to the dugout with us, but of course, his ban has now stretched for more than thirty years.

There are many ways to evaluate Rose's life and career, opinions that have been shaped by his actions, on and off the field. In my view, he is a Hall-of-Fame player. I know someone permanently banned from baseball can't be inducted into the Hall. But I think Pete deserves to be in the Hall for setting the all-time record of 4,256 hits while playing the game with unbridled passion and joy. He also holds the records for most games played (3,562), most plate appearances (15,890), and most at bats (14,053); he won a Most Valuable Player Award and finished in the top ten for the MVP nine other times; and he played on three World Series winners. I grew up watching Pete and idolized him, and then I had the chance to play with him and be managed by him. In the early months of my career, he was so superior to me and many major-league hitters. He was an elite hitter and a memorable player. And, for me, that's how I think of him: Pete will always be a Hall of Famer.

Tommy Helms, Rose's close friend and our first-base coach, replaced Rose and became the interim manager. We wan-dered through the final five weeks of the season, a season that I will always remember for the wrong reasons. I witnessed the downfall of one of my heroes and someone who had a profound impact on me as a hitter.

———⊸⊶———

The first time Lou Piniella spoke as the new manager of the Reds and the man who essentially succeeded Rose, he was blunt. Piniella surveyed our roster and saw "a wealth of good, young arms" and didn't envision that he was "going into a rebuilding process." We had won 75 games and finished fifth in the National League West in 1989, but Lou said we were a team that could win a World Series.

I liked hearing those positive words, and I agreed with Lou. We did have enough talent to win a championship, but we had underachieved during a messy season. The Reds had also finished second in the division in 1985, 1986, 1987, and 1988, and Piniella wanted to change that mindset of being second fiddle. Immediately, Lou brought a winning attitude and New York class and toughness into our clubhouse. I think it was Lou's intention to call us out and send a message from day one. And that shouldn't have shocked me or anyone else.

Before joining the Reds, Piniella had spent sixteen years with the Yankees as a feisty player, a feisty coach, a feisty manager (twice), and a feisty general manager, and he had also been a scout and a broadcaster, too. Yes, Lou was perpetually feisty, and he was also a baseball lifer who desperately wanted to win. The combative Piniella was a vital contributor on the Yankees' championship teams in 1977 and 1978, and he hit .291 with 1,705 hits in his eighteen-year career. Honestly, with the fiery, emotional way Piniella behaved, he kind of reminded me of me. And I guess the feeling was mutual: "Paul was more talented than I was," Piniella said. "He was bigger, and he was stronger, and the ball jumped off his bat. He wanted to be as good as he could possibly be, and he fought himself a lot. He reminded me of myself."

After a 1989 season in which I hit .276 with a .346 on-base percentage, a .446 slugging percentage, 15 homers, and 74 runs batted in, I was ready to continue to assert myself as a middle-of-the-order hitter on a very good team. Players often claim they don't care what other players say about them. But there are times that's not true, especially if it's a dynamic pitcher like Orel Hershiser.

Hershiser was the best pitcher in the world in 1988 as he was named the MVP of the World Series when the Dodgers defeated the Athletics. He also set a record during the regular season by throwing fifty-nine straight scoreless innings. He was hellish to face because his two-seam fastball looked like it was about to drill me in the hip before it broke dramatically from the left to the right and into the strike zone. He was a superstar. And before his first start against us in 1989, Orel gave a scouting report on the Reds' lineup and included me as one of the players who could do damage and perhaps even take him deep. It was a basic mention, but after I read it, I was pleased that Hershiser considered me even a hint of a threat. If a great pitcher was talking about me as someone he needed to be aware of, I thought, maybe I was a pretty solid hitter.

Heading into 1990, I thought about Hershiser's one-year-old comment and his words made me work even harder so that all pitchers would view me in the same way. I wanted to continue belting line drives and I wanted to achieve my goals of hitting .300 and driving in 100 runs. But something happened on the way to chasing those special numbers. Piniella, my new manager and my new boss, was looming around the batting cage, and he wanted to change the way I hit.

I had immense respect for Lou's knowledge, and I know he wanted to make me a better hitter, but it was very difficult for me to change my approach. I had successfully climbed to the major leagues by hitting a certain way, and it didn't make sense to overhaul what I had already done. These days, I know there are numerous stories of hitters (like J. D. Martinez and Justin Turner) who have flourished by altering their swings and their mechanics to hit the ball in the air more frequently. I understand and appreciate that kind of commitment to succeed. But I was comfortable with my way of hitting line drives.

My thought process as a hitter was to stay on top of the ball, stay through the ball, and hit the ball hard. If there was a videotape of my swing from the side, it would have shown a level swing as I tried to hit on top of the ball and brought my bat through the zone. But eventually, my bat would follow through over my shoulder and I would finish with a slight uppercut. That's how I was comfortable swinging and that's how I produced line drives.

But Lou wanted me to stay anchored on my back leg, use a weight shift to turn on pitches and elevate them, and knock them out of the ballpark. It was frustrating because it contradicted everything my father had taught me. To me, line drives weren't just good. Line drives were great. But Lou thought a hitter with my size and strength could and should hit with more power, and he wanted me to adopt some of his methods. By the way, those methods had been very beneficial for Don Mattingly, which I will explain in the next chapter. I was uneasy with making those modifications. They didn't work for me. But Lou was persistent. "I kept telling him: you can be better than what you are," Piniella explained. "Obviously, you're good. But you can be better. I really saw the possibility of greatness in him. He was a big, strong guy who could hit the ball with power to all fields. He didn't strike out that much for a big guy. And, like I said, he could run. Basically, I thought he could be even better."

Lou challenged me, which was appropriate because I believe every player should be challenged to improve. And Lou had an immediate impact on our club. We began the year 9-0, cruised to a 33-12 record, and had a ten-game cushion in the division by early June. In fact, we were in first place for all 178 days of that regular season.

In my first postseason, I was anxious again because the stage and the stakes are bigger. But I finished the regular season feeling confident about my swing, and I went 8 for 17 (.471 average) as we throttled the Pittsburgh Pirates in six games to win the National League Championship Series. In Game 6, I smacked a run-scoring single to drive in our first run. In the seventh inning, I was scheduled to face left-hander Zane Smith, and Lou used Luis Quiñones, a .241 hitter for us that season, to pinch-hit for me. I wasn't happy about it. I had been our most prolific hitter in the series and now Lou had replaced me. I trudged through the dugout and grabbed a cup of water, just to have something to do. But the right-handed hitting

Quiñones delivered a tie-breaking single, and we won 2-1. Afterward, I said Piniella had made a "gutsy" move in removing me. Maybe *gutsy* was the wrong word. Maybe I should have called it strategic—I did finish my career 2 for 16 against Smith. Anyway, Piniella's decision worked, and we were going to the World Series.

Piniella continued to make some bold choices to help us startle Henderson, McGwire, Canseco, and the mighty A's, and I was in the middle of that, too. With Oakland's Dave Stewart clinging to a 1-0 lead in Game 4, Barry Larkin singled in the eighth inning. Herm Winningham followed by bunting on an 0-2 pitch and beating it out for a single. I was hitting third in our lineup, and this was a perfect opportunity for me to knock in some runs against a right-handed pitcher. But that didn't matter to Lou. My teammate Chris Sabo told me Lou hustled over to him in the dugout and asked, "Can O'Neill bunt?" Sabo said, "I guess so." And that exchange led to me receiving a bunt sign, even though I had one sacrifice bunt in 564 plate appearances that season. My bunt trickled back to Stewart. He fielded it and should have easily had me at first, but his throw was wide. We had the bases loaded with no outs. An RBI groundout and a sacrifice fly produced 2 runs and we stole a 2-1 win.

Can you imagine the outcry if a manager instructed his number three batter to bunt in that situation in 2022? As unorthodox as it might seem now, it worked. Lou's small-ball tactics helped win us that game and his fingerprints are all over that four-game sweep of the A's. We shocked the defending champions in what was considered one of the greatest upsets in World Series history. Lou brought an intensity into the Reds' clubhouse and was superb in guiding us to the organization's first title since the Big Red Machine days. Ironically, he was on the Yankee team that lost to the 1976 Reds, Cincinnati's last champions.

One out away from winning that first World Series, my knees were bent and my upper body was leaning forward in right field. I vividly recall thinking about the beauty and the improbability of what we were about to achieve. When Carney Lansford hit a soft pop-up to the right side off Randy Myers, I was hoping it would carry to me so I could catch the final out. But the ball didn't make it that far, as first baseman Todd Benzinger retreated several steps and caught it in foul territory. Benzinger raised his arms in the air, the relievers from the right-field bullpen rushed onto the field, and I joined them in the celebration. We had done it. We had dethroned the A's and won it all.

There is no more fulfilling feeling than winning a World Series title, especially while playing for your hometown team. I was twenty-seven years old and my team, the team I cherished as a kid, had reached the pinnacle. Those championship memories are everlasting and have allowed me to overlook that I went 1 for 12 with five walks in the series.

A few days after we returned home, about ten thousand delirious fans attended a championship parade at Fountain Square in downtown Cincinnati. It was a rainy day, but that didn't silence the fans who chanted, "Sweep! Sweep! Sweep!" There were thirty convertibles that ferried players, coaches, Piniella, and team officials about five blocks through the city.

I know it was a sweet experience for Lou. He had been fired twice by the Yankees and he was a boyhood friend (and long-time rival) of Tony La Russa, Oakland's manager, as both of them grew up in Tampa.

Toward the end of the 1990 season, Lou told reporters something he had already told me: he believed I could hit 35 homers the next season. At that point, my career high in homers was 16. Our lineup didn't have many power options, and Lou thought I would best help the team if I could be that big, brawny guy who blasted 35 homers. I appreciate how Lou felt about me and the confidence he had in me, but to him, being a better hitter meant doing it his way, and that didn't work for me.

"I tried to get him to weight shift," Piniella said. "I loved the fact that he had a really nice leg kick and gathered it on his back foot. We tried to get him to lateral shift a little more. Tony Pérez worked with him. He was hitting coach over there in Cincinnati. And Tony was good at what he did. Tony kept telling me, 'Push him. Push him to be better. That's the only way you're going to get him to be better.' And that's exactly what I tried to do. And, at times, we'd have a little run-in here and there. But it was nothing that lasted for more than just a moment."

Actually, I remember Lou being more of the protagonist in pushing me. Tony does, too.

"I know Lou put a lot of pressure on him," Pérez said. "You can ask Paul about that. I was talking to Lou about it and I said, 'Leave it alone. Let the guy play.' But Lou was different. Lou wanted to win so much. He wanted to win so bad. When we would lose a few games, he went crazy. But that's the way he was. But sometimes with hitters like Paul, you have to leave it alone because he will hit. But he will hit his way, not somebody else's way."

Tony was right. I would hit for the Reds, but I had to hit in a way that satisfied me. When a hitter tries to do something that collides with everything he has been taught, that will lead to some confusing and exasperating at bats. There were definitely some stressful moments with Lou, and that relationship worsened when I was playing for the Yankees and he was managing the Mariners. Every so often, I would have a pitch aimed at my neck. But while we were together with the Reds, I know that Lou believed I could accomplish a lot in the batter's box, and that's why he pushed me. I am grateful for that. But did his ideas help me? No, they really didn't.

Basically, Piniella thought he could devise a way for me to hit more homers and have more success against certain left-handed pitchers. He felt that I sometimes stayed back on my heels too long in my swing. He actually instructed me to wear lifts in my spikes to boost my heels as I was swinging! I have never heard of any hitter doing that. I felt like I was trying to hit with high-heeled shoes on. As Piniella was trying to get me to be more balanced, I felt more clumsy.

"I thought his weight was back on his heels from time to time and that would make him pull off the ball even more," Piniella said. "We worked a lot on balance, approach, and shifting the weight in his legs. With him, we worked on staying right-center and left-center with the ball. Not just trying to pull the ball. Work from left-center to right-center. He had good power to both alleys. I had some good hitters with the Reds and I had enough confidence in Paul to hit him third in my lineup."

The thing is, I hit 28 homers in 1991 as I tried to be more of the power hitter Lou wanted me to be, but I was miserable. Besides the home run total, I struck out 107 times, a career high, and I only hit .256, tied for the second-lowest mark in my career. I considered myself a better hitter than that, but I felt like I was searching for my swing all season long. Trying to hit home runs wasn't my thing. Did I want to hit the ball in the air? Of course, I did. But I wanted to hit line drives.

One of Piniella's most insightful comments about me was that I didn't have the temperament to be a 40-home-run hitter. He was right. The problem is, Lou said that long after I had retired! To even dream of bashing 40 homers, my average would have to suffer and that would have made me go ballistic. Listen, I understand there are players in today's game who hit 40 homers and never blink about striking out 200 times and hitting about .220. If that's the right recipe for them and their team, I guess that's fine. But that never would have worked for me. While it took Lou too long to realize this, I wasn't that type of hitter.

"To be a 40-to-45-homer guy, you have to have the right temperament," Piniella said. "Yeah, you've got to be strong. You have to have all of the ingredients that go into being that kind of power hitter. But you have to have the temperament that allows you to be OK with making more outs and striking out and hitting balls 415 feet to center field and making an out, as opposed to hitting a ball in the gap and driving in a run with a double."

Interestingly, Lou also said I reminded him of himself, because he didn't have that type of temperament, either. Of course, that makes me a little crazy—why, then, did Piniella implore me to hit that way? Again, I know Lou saw talent in me and he tried to cultivate it. Lou repeatedly talked about my size and the way the ball jumped off my bat, and to him, that should have translated into more homers.

But I was so disappointed, even embarrassed when I struck out, because that meant I had been beaten by the pitcher. If I hit a ball hard, even if it was an out, I felt that I had at least connected and made the pitcher sweat a bit. To swing and miss a lot and be a home-run-or-bust kind of guy? No way, that wasn't my game.

By the way, I understand that members of some analytics departments might argue a strikeout is just like any other out, because they count the same. But as a proud hitter who judged myself on what I accomplished in every at bat, I have never seen it that way. When a hitter puts the ball in play, he has a chance to make something happen for his team. Strikeouts are a waste.

"I will tell you something about O'Neill: He didn't want to be embarrassed by striking out," said Buck Showalter, my former Yankees manager who now manages the Mets. "In today's game, strikeouts are accepted. It's part of the game. When O'Neill struck out? You didn't want to be in the dugout. You didn't want to be there when he came back because you would say, 'OK. Here comes the explosion.' I would be saying, 'Just please get a hit. I don't want to see that explosion again.'

Or, at least if it was the third out, he would have to go out to the outfield."

Under Piniella, it was such a tug-of-war between us because I knew what I needed to do. Pérez kept telling me that he told Piniella to let me hit the way I preferred. So did Ken Griffey Sr., who was on the 1990 team before being traded to the Mariners. One day, Senior pulled me aside and said, "I've told these guys you're a great hitter. Go out there and hit the way you're going to hit." Like Pérez, who was a Hall of Famer, the sweet-swinging Griffey was another player I had idolized, so it was meaningful to receive their support. I guess I wasn't insane for feeling this way and being stubborn about my approach.

I had many closed-door meetings with Lou, some that escalated into shouting sessions. While Piniella admits, "Paul probably got a little frustrated with me, at times," I never felt a lack of support from him. I had to remind myself that Piniella wanted me to be great. We just had different views on the proper route to making that happen.

Fittingly or unfittingly, both Lou and I had our final run with the Reds together in 1992. We went from being teammates to being adversaries, as I was traded to the Yankees and Piniella became the manager of the Mariners. As much friction as existed between us in Cincinnati, that combusted when we were in opposite dugouts. And I wasn't the one igniting those flames and making that happen.

Based on the way Lou's pitchers threw up and in to me, it was obvious that Lou wanted to make me as uneasy as possible. Piniella knew my hitting style as well as anyone. He knew that I liked to extend my arms to hit pitches that were on the middle or the outside part of the plate, so Lou's pitchers went high and tight to back me off the plate. Now there's a right way to throw inside (by making a batter move his feet) and there's a wrong way to do that (by aiming it closer to his head).

The tension between us and our teams bubbled over on August 28, 1996, when Tim Davis threw a pitch that was up and in during the eighth inning of a lopsided game. I sprawled to the ground and glared at Davis for a few moments because I believed the pitch was intentionally trying to plunk me. When I stood up and returned to the batter's box, I told John Marzano, their catcher, why I was incensed with the pitch.

That's when the side show started.

We tussled and Marzano uncorked a right-handed punch, but I ducked out of the way and tackled him to the ground. As we rolled around near the plate, both benches emptied. The typical baseball "non-brawl" occurred—the players circled each other on the field, with a little pushing and a lot of posturing taking place.

And just when it seemed as if order had been restored, Darryl Strawberry, who was six feet six and about 220 pounds of wiry muscles, nearly went at it with two Seattle pitchers. The scuffle had resumed. The fight delayed the game for ten minutes, and five players, including me and Marzano, were ejected. The next day, Straw, who seemed a bit bruised and weary, jokingly told me he might have to sit out the next skirmish.

Obviously, I felt this was all Seattle's fault. Of course, Lou saw it differently: "You know I get tired of this guy crying every time we come inside on him," said Piniella, as he smoked a cigarette after the game. "I get sick and tired of it. I'm sure other pitchers come inside, and his reaction is the same. When you see a player get frustrated, lose his concentration, and go crazy like that, what the heck do you think is going to happen?"

There was no doubt I had been targeted in that game. It wasn't the first time it happened, and Lou's intimidation tactics bothered the heck out of me. "I'm getting sick and tired of this," I said after the game. "You've seen it. It's been going on for four years. It's the same garbage. This is bad."

My relationship with Piniella was surely a complicated one, a relationship that featured two intense competitors. I was always civil and respectful with Lou, and again, I have always believed he wanted me to be a tremendous hitter. Eventually, both of us ended up in the broadcast booth and even announced some Yankees games together. Talk about a situation I never would have envisioned while busting out of the box after another uncomfortable pitch and glaring into the dugout at him. Well, the lesson from this relationship is: two very competitive, very passionate, and very stubborn baseball men aren't always going to agree with each other. Lou and I proved that.

In 1992, I didn't know Lou was leaving the Reds after the season, but I was too worried about my own situation to worry about anyone else's. I felt like I was at a crossroads. I was a starting outfielder for the Reds and I had a World Series ring. But I finished the season in horrendous fashion: a .230 average, 3 homers, and 16 runs batted in across the last seven weeks. I had to be better. A lot better. I had been pondering the idea of perfecting my leg kick and I told myself 1993 was going to be different.

It turns out I was right. It was different. I just didn't know how different, or that a new city was about to become my baseball home.

CHAPTER 3

Playing with Two Icons: Donnie and Derek

Nervous. Unsettled. Tense. Concerned. Those were the feelings I had after I was traded from the Cincinnati Reds to the New York Yankees on November 3, 1992—a deal that changed my life and my family's life for the better in a million ways. But when I first heard that I was traded, I was upset and uncertain. And my wife, Nevalee, was even more distraught. Nevalee and I met when we were five years old and lived in the same neighborhood, so she had experienced every moment of my life, not just my baseball life, with me. This moment jolted us.

The Reds delivered the news by leaving a message on my home answering machine. Yes, it happened so long ago that we still received voice mail that way. After we listened to each word slowly and carefully, Nevalee was weeping and I was in shock. I had heard a few rumors about possibly being traded, but it was still jarring. We wondered how this move would impact our family and we also thought about how challenging a place New York would be.

I mean…New York? Big, noisy, and intimidating New York? I hate to admit this, but do you know what I knew about New York? I knew that the Reds typically stayed at the Hyatt Grand Central hotel on East Forty-Second Street in Manhattan, and I knew how to travel from my room to the lobby to the street to catch the team bus to the Mets ballpark in Queens. I didn't leave the hotel too often when the Reds played in New York. Greenwich Village? The Upper East Side? The South Bronx? The subway? Those were foreign, almost scary places to me.

While we were still processing the news, Gene Michael, the Yankees' general manager, called and put me at ease about my new challenge and made me excited about the idea of playing for the Yankees. Michael—who was known as Stick because he was lean enough to hide behind a foul pole—talked fast, but more importantly, he spoke enthusiastically and passionately about making the Yankees a winning team. I could sense how much he and the Yankees wanted me, and that meant a lot.

"You're going to be the perfect fit for us," Stick told me. "We're in the process of turning this thing around and you're going to be a big part of making that happen. We need a left-handed hitter like you at Yankee Stadium." Hitting. Once Stick mentioned hitting and discussed how I would fit in, he had uttered the enticing words that quickly got my attention. Stick told me that he appreciated how I hit the ball to all fields and that the Yankees didn't need me to be a prolific home-run hitter. That was as important as anything he could have said to me that day, even more important than where he thought I should live in New York. Instantly, I was envisioning how I would dig my spikes into the batter's box at the Stadium. I knew that my new organization was going to let me swing the bat the way I wanted, not the way Lou Piniella wanted me to hit with the Reds.

The Yankees, who are the most storied and successful franchise in baseball history, hadn't been competitive for several seasons. They lost 95 games in 1990, they lost 91 in 1991, and after Buck Showalter replaced Stump Merrill as manager in 1992, they went 76-86. But as I would soon learn, Stick and Buck had a plan for changing the culture around the Yankees. They wanted quality veterans who were accountable and who cared more about the team than themselves, they wanted durable pitchers who didn't complain, they wanted to fortify the team through the farm system, and they wanted the Yankees to be a destination for free agents again. Within six weeks of my trade, the Yankees signed third baseman Wade Boggs and pitcher Jimmy Key to free-agent contracts and acquired pitcher Jim Abbott from the Angels. Stick also tried valiantly to sign superstars Barry Bonds and Greg Maddux, but Bonds demanded a sixth year, so the Yankees pulled their offer, and Maddux took less money to join the Atlanta Braves. Despite all that, Stick and Buck kept making shrewd decisions and proved how serious they were about this turnaround.

When Stick watched me with the Reds, I'm so thankful he saw the hitter he believed I could be. I could spray line drives all around the stadium, I could play a Gold Glove–caliber defense in the outfield, and I could even poke some shots into the right-field seats, but I wasn't a swing-from-your-heels home-run hitter. I hit 28 homers and had an .827 OPS with the 1991 Reds, both career highs at the time, and, obviously that was a memorable season. But I also hit .256, I struck out a career-worst 107 times, and I repeatedly felt uncomfortable because of my hitting disagreements with Lou.

"Stick was great at figuring out that someone who might have been perceived as having a problem elsewhere, well, the problem really wasn't that big of a deal," said Showalter. "Basically, Paul O'Neill and Lou Piniella had problems. Stick and Lou were close friends and Stick knew Lou like the back of his hand. Stick told me that he also knew me well and he thought that Paul and I would be perfect together. I thought so, too."

I never considered myself a problem player in Cincinnati, but Buck pretty much nailed it in describing how the trade occurred. Heck, even Lou, who left the Reds one month before they traded me to New York, told Stick that he should make the deal: "After I had left there and I went to manage in Seattle or wherever I was, Stick called me and told me he could trade O'Neill for Roberto Kelly," Piniella said. "I said, 'What are you waiting for? This guy will be a natural in Yankee Stadium with the short porch. The fans in New York like a little fire and they like a guy who shows his emotions. I told him the fans in New York would love this guy.'"

As Stick discussed how the Yankees envisioned their 1993 lineup, he mentioned Bernie Williams, Danny Tartabull, Don Mattingly, Wade Boggs, Mike Stanley, and me being the mainstays. Stick compared me to Mattingly by saying that Donnie liked to smash hits to every part of the field and considered himself more of a doubles hitter than a home-run hitter. I was pleasantly surprised to hear Stick compare my hitting to Mattingly's style. From afar, I had always admired Mattingly as a hitter. He was strong, smart, and resilient and always seemed to have a dirty uniform. I've never seen a player who looked better with lamp black under his eyes than Mattingly. Obviously, that had nothing to do with the type of extraordinary hitter he was, but Donnie, to me, always looked like the player who would be cast in a movie about a superb and selfless player.

In the casting meeting for my imaginary movie, one movie person with scant baseball knowledge would say, "We need a guy who looks like he eats, sleeps, and dreams baseball, who his teammates respect and admire, and who the fans adore because of how hard he plays and how much he cares." Then I imagine the knowledgeable baseball people who were in the meeting would all respond, "So, we need Mattingly."

I needed Mattingly, too—I desperately wanted to talk hitting with him. I didn't call him Don or Donnie too often. As a sign of respect, I called Mattingly "Cap" because he was the Yankees' devoted captain, he was our leader, and he was the player who had done it all and seen it all in New York. Mattingly won the 1985 Most Valuable Player Award, he had won an armful of Gold Glove Awards for his slick play at first, and he had experienced the good and the bad of playing in New York. Tabloid hero one day. Tabloid goat the next. But with Donnie, it was mostly very, very good. In my opinion, Mattingly was the best player in the majors from 1984 to 1987, when his season averages were: .337 batting average, 30 homers, 121 runs batted in, 211 hits, and an OPS of .941. He might have been the best player in other seasons, too, but in those seasons, it wasn't a contest. He finished fifth, first, second, and seventh in MVP voting in those four seasons.

I loved to discuss the intricacies of hitting with Donnie because he was a student of the game (and a teacher, too), he was a left-handed batter like me, he had seen more of the American League pitchers than me, and he had immense experience to draw on. If a certain pitcher threw Mattingly a slider in a 3-1 count, I wanted to know about it and I wanted to know what Donnie thought about that. Now, I must stress, we were definitely different hitters—he crouched more in his stance and used a weight shift to produce power, while I stood more upright and used my leg kick for timing—but there were enough similarities for us to share notes and make each other better.

The clubhouse at old Yankee Stadium was on the first-base side of the field, a haven of about forty lockers stretched along all four walls with white frieze trim filling the room. When I exited the clubhouse, I would walk straight ahead and down a runway to get to the field. There was a blue-and-white sign hanging from the ceiling with a Joe DiMaggio quote that said, "I want to thank the Good Lord for making me a Yankee." I strolled down that dugout runway for nine seasons and each trip was more exciting than the last one.

But if I made a right turn after leaving the clubhouse, that path would take me to my second favorite spot at the Stadium: the indoor batting cages under the right-field stands. After making the right out of the clubhouse, I would walk along a narrow hallway—which was about twelve feet wide and had ceilings so low that I sometimes felt I would hit my head—and kept walking until I reached a dead end. I made the walk a thousand times, bat and batting gloves in hand and an urgency to my step. I loved to hit, but not just in games. I loved to talk hitting, practice hitting, and think hitting.

Guess who was always in the batting cage with me? The Captain.

Inside those black-netted cages, there was a thin, green turf surface and one pitching machine that was known as an Iron Mike. The blue paint seemed to peel off the walls in this room a little more each day. There were cracks in the ceiling and there never seemed to be enough folding chairs for all of the waiting hitters. But for me and Cap, this modest, dingy place was our sanctuary.

I didn't like to hit against the Iron Mike because I preferred to see the baseball coming out of the pitcher's hand. Any time I hit off the machine, I would inevitably lunge to time the pitch that was pumping out of the mechanical arm and that would disrupt my mechanics. Instead, I would take my swings against a batting practice pitcher because I wanted to see his motion and release. Nick Testa, one of the pitchers, was a short, muscular man in his midsixties who probably threw about 60 miles per hour, but I didn't mind the Little League velocity. I was just more comfortable hitting against a pitcher.

Hour after hour in the cage, I would listen to the ball fly off Cap's bat. Whack! Whack! Whack! Because of the concrete walls surrounding the cage, the room had satisfying acoustics for hitters. There's nothing better than hearing that booming sound reverberating off the walls after hitting a baseball because it made every hitter feel like he had crushed the pitch, even if he hadn't.

Mattingly's work was like my work. We were relentless, with dozens of swings producing so many baseballs soaring around the cage before rolling to a stop. Then we would pick up the baseballs and do it all over again. We would tease each other after lousy swings, or Mattingly would accuse me of yelling at a fake umpire when I didn't swing, but it was serious work because we were making ourselves better. Donnie was a nineteenth-round pick out of high school in 1979, and honestly, the odds are against nineteenth-round picks making it to the majors. I think Cap carried that chip on his shoulder for his entire career, because his work ethic was a thing of beauty.

I learned a lot from watching Donnie work and from just talking about hitting with him. We both agreed on the importance of having a two-strike approach. Once a batter gets to two strikes in a count, he must adjust because a pitcher can bury him with one nasty pitch. That doesn't mean a batter has to automatically choke up three inches on the bat. But it does mean that a batter should have a less aggressive swing that's designed to make contact and drive the ball. The hitter should try to focus on the middle of the field and not think that he has to pull the ball. I know that's not the way most hitters approach hitting in the modern game. There are a lot of home-run swings on 0-0 counts, 0-1 counts, and 0-2 counts. Again, as I've said, I understand it because that's the way the game has trended, and home runs are king.

It was obvious that both Donnie and I believed in the

value of putting the ball in play. Like every hitter, I loved the idea of hitting a ball 420 feet for a homer, but I needed to do everything perfectly for that to happen. I also believed in the importance of piecing together a productive at bat and not simply flailing at an 0-2 curve because I was trying to bash it 420 feet. The smarter approach against that type of pitch was to stay back, stay balanced, and maybe smack that pitch for a line drive single.

Obviously, it sounds so simple to say a hitter needs to get a good pitch to hit. That's understood, right? That's a basic part of hitting, right? Of course, it is, but that's something Donnie emphasized in the intelligent way that he attacked pitchers and took advantage of their mistakes. How many times does a batter expand the strike zone with two strikes and get himself out? How many times does a batter's overzealousness early in an at bat cause him to lose the at bat and essentially give the pitcher a free out? It happens all the time. When Mattingly and I worked in the cage, we stressed the importance of doing damage on that one hittable pitch (or two) we were certain to get in each at bat.

When we left the cage and took batting practice outdoors before games, I was focused on staying on top of the ball and hitting baseballs from gap to gap. During the last round of BP, batters would usually lighten the mood and play home-run derby. It was a fun competition to see who could blast the most baseballs over the fence. Call me a grouch, but I hated that game. I didn't like to shoot for homers because I thought that would adversely tweak the swing I had been working on for the last few hours.

As much as I learned from Cap, I also learned some things that I wouldn't do or couldn't do. Mattingly was so confident in his ability to hit left-handed pitchers that he would look for sliders that were sailing right at him. Since the pitch looked like it was about to hit him, Donnie knew it was probably going to have late-breaking action and spin over the plate and become a strike. So, he would actually wait for those spinning sliders that seemed destined to hit him and he would punish them. If the slider looked like it was going to be a strike, he would lay off the pitch because it was likely to spin out of the strike zone. I understood that concept, but I couldn't hit that way. When I saw a pitch coming toward me, even if I thought it was a spinning slider, my natural reaction was to flinch. So, I couldn't condition myself to get geared up to swing at that pitch.

Interestingly enough, Donnie's evolution as a hitter was influenced by Piniella after they first became teammates in Cap's rookie season in 1982. Then Piniella later became Mattingly's hitting coach and his manager with the Yankees. Cap wasn't the biggest guy in the clubhouse at about five feet eleven and 185 pounds, but he was strong. Lou tutored Donnie on shifting his weight and driving the ball so that he could take advantage of the right-field porch at the Stadium.

Donnie explained how Lou taught him to get more power out of his swing by using his whole body as he drove into the ball. That meant using his lower half (hips and legs), upper half (back and shoulders), and of course, his hands to power his swing. Donnie would shift his weight from his back side to his front side as he swung and then drive through the ball.

This weight shift swing was about precise timing because moving too quickly would cause him to tip forward and moving too slowly would cause him to dip backward. But as I watched Donnie swing in a seamless fashion, it was obvious that he had perfected it. From a side view, he looked perfectly balanced. He wasn't fighting to get to the ball, he didn't have to pull his hands closer to his body, and he wasn't lunging or lagging.

My conversations with Mattingly extended from the cage to the clubhouse to the dugout and even to the movie theater. The movie theater? Yes, the movie theater. On one West Coast road trip, we had a day game in Oakland and Cap and I ended up going to a movie that night. Imagine that—Mattingly, the great Yankees' captain, and me cruising into the theater to grab a couple of buckets of popcorn and catch the latest flick. Although I don't remember what movie we saw, I do remember that I was morose because I was in the middle of an 0 for 10 slump that felt like an 0 for 100. As I sometimes did, I was moaning about my swing and how I wasn't helping the team. I turned to my captain for help.

"Hey, Cap," I asked, "am I ever going to get another hit?"

Mattingly, his popcorn awaiting, looked at me very seriously and stayed silent for a few seconds. I figured he was going to tell me that I was swinging the bat better than I realized and that I would eventually bust out of the slump. But instead, Mattingly said, "Another hit for you? Nah. Probably not. I'm not seeing that in your future."

The Captain was a jokester! Of course, I roared and registered my first laugh before the movie previews had even started. No one else would have probably been that blunt with me, but Mattingly and I had shared so many discussions about success and failure as hitters that he knew how to tweak me. If anyone else had said that, I wouldn't have been as jovial about it. But Cap had the freedom to do that because he was reminding me how foolish I sounded. I watched the movie with a renewed hope that somehow and some way, I would get another hit.

In my second game as a Yankee in 1993, I was benched against a left-hander named Jeff Mutis, who was making his sixth major league start. Ouch. That stung. As forthcoming as Stick had been with me, he never admitted he was worried about me getting off to a sluggish start. Because of that fear, Stick wanted Buck to rest me against certain lefties. Double ouch.

"With Paul, I had the number .215 in my head," Showalter said. "Stick kept saying '.215, .215, .215,' because that's what Paul hit against lefties with the Reds. He didn't want to see him struggle when he first got to New York so we sat him against some lefties."

Showalter was a baseball genius, a manager who was extremely organized and who never looked flustered in the dugout. Buck was so detailed that he could elaborate on which team's grounds crew watered the field too much and which team's grounds crew kept the grass shorter than it should have been. We had meetings about our signs, meetings about our strategies, and I think we had meetings about our next meetings. Personally, I also had some one-on-one meetings with Buck, mostly when I wanted to know why I wasn't playing against a particular lefty.

My goal was to be a major leaguer, which I had achieved, but that goal included the very important element of being an everyday player. I hated sitting on the bench. I didn't like days off. And I despised sitting against a lefty because there was a manager telling me I wasn't a good enough hitter that day. When I stared at a lineup card on the clubhouse door and didn't see my name in it, I viewed it as a challenge. I wanted to prove everyone wrong.

Sure, I knew that my statistics against lefties weren't fantastic in Cincinnati, although I did hit a decent .259 against them on our 1990 championship team. But for me, the way to continue to improve against lefties was through repetition and by facing as many lefties as possible. I embraced that test and it annoyed me when one of my managers didn't feel as confident in me as I felt in myself.

I never understood how a right-handed batter could look uncomfortable against a righty pitcher and flail away at a sweeping slider, and it's just considered one bad at bat. It's rare for anyone to criticize a righty batter for not hitting righty pitchers. But if a lefty batter opened up his front shoulder too quickly and looked equally awkward in whiffing on a slider, there's an immediate outcry of, "Wow. That guy can't hit lefty pitchers." I hated that double standard. While I tried to avoid it, I put more pressure on myself when I faced lefties because I knew I was being evaluated with every at bat.

These days, starters don't pitch as deep into games and there are so many bullpen matchups that teams strive to exploit. I wouldn't have wanted to be the starting player who was consistently removed for a pinch hitter in the late innings because a manager didn't think I could produce against the latest power reliever. In the current game, velocity rules, with virtually every bullpen boasting pitchers who throw about 100 miles per hour. When I played, I faced a lot of crafty lefty relievers like Jesse Orosco and Paul Assenmacher, pitchers who would attack with breaking pitches. At times, I think the crafty lefties were more difficult for me to hit than power-throwing pitchers. With the pitchers who were mostly throwing fastballs, I just kept telling myself, "Turn it up a little. Be ready to start your swing a bit earlier. Do damage when you see something in the zone."

No matter how persistently I presented my case for playing every day to Buck, he still benched me against some lefties and it aggravated me. He knew it. I knew it. Stick knew it. But the manager made out the lineup card, not me. Sometimes, I stewed in the dugout and waited for an opportunity. "He was so pissed at me about platooning, and at times not playing him," said Showalter. "I told him, 'You're going to get your chance. There will be situations where I use you against a lefty.' And I also told him, 'When I do give you a chance, just imagine my face is on the baseball and try to hit me right between the bleeping eyes.'"

Wearing his ubiquitous Yankees jacket, Showalter had a pregame routine of marching around the field to talk with his players. His initial stop would always be at first base with Mattingly, a savvy move. Donnie knew the pulse of the team better than anyone and he was a great sounding board for Showalter, his former minor-league teammate. In addition, by consulting with Mattingly, the most revered player on the team, Showalter reinforced to the rest of us that he and Donnie were in this together and that we should be, too.

I was a team player, too, but that didn't mean I was averse to some pouting. I wanted to play. On the days when I wasn't starting, I didn't want to have a deep conversation with Buck. As he left Mattingly and walked toward me in right field, I would make his job tougher and amble to center field to shag fly balls. And when the determined Buck followed me to center, I would take one, two, three steps to my right and just keep shuffling toward left field. I know it seems childish, but I wasn't happy about sitting, and in those moments, nothing he said was going to pacify me. "I knew he was pissed," Buck said. "He figured out what I was trying to do and he'd keep walking from right to center to left to avoid me. He would be making circles in the outfield and I'd have to chase him around. I would get closer to him and I would hear him say, 'What does that stumpy little bleep want? He must know I'm pissed.' I did know it and I was trying to explain myself to him."

I've made it clear that I always wanted to play against lefties. Always. But there was one game in 1993 in which lefty Bob Patterson was on the mound for the Texas Rangers, and based on Showalter's previous decisions, I assumed he would pinch-hit for me. Plus, I couldn't always pick up the baseball out of Patterson's hand and ended up 3 for 20 against him in my career. I never looked toward the dugout to see if a batter was about to replace me, but this time, I did. And Buck didn't budge. He didn't wave me back and summon a pinch hitter.

Buck said I looked at him with an expression that said, "If you don't pinch-hit for me against this dude, then I will be pissed." He didn't, and I struck out.

"We butted heads a few times," said Showalter about our relationship. "Paul was stubborn. He was a hard head. The same thing that made him good also made him kind of tough to manage, at times."

I knew what I had to do to be successful against lefties: I had to stay in there, meaning my front shoulder had to stay closer to my body until I was ready to unleash my swing. If I opened up my shoulder and started my swing too early, my upper body would fly open toward the right side, I would be off-balance, and I wouldn't be able to get to any pitches that were middle or away.

While it's easy for me to say that, it's not easy to do it. Naturally, I wanted to pile up the at bats against lefties to improve (and prove) myself. There's a definite toughness that comes with hanging close to the plate against a lefty who is throwing 97 miles per hour and not starting your swing too early, even though you're not always picking up the ball well. It can be frightening, and it can be nerve-racking, but it's the only way to hit those power lefties.

One of my most rewarding examples of that approach came against the Mariners during Game 2 of the 1995 American League Division Series. The Mariners, of course, were managed by Piniella, my former manager and the man who longed to make me uncomfortable by having his pitchers buzz me inside. Down by a run in the seventh inning, I was facing Norm Charlton, who was my friend and former teammate with the Reds. Norm combined with Rob Dibble and Randy Myers to form the "Nasty Boys," a trio of relievers who dominated for the Reds when we won the 1990 World Series. I knew Norm well. He threw hard, harder, and hardest. In the regular season and postseason, I was 4 for 21 against him in my career.

With two outs in the inning, I just kept telling myself to stay back, stay balanced, and try not to get too excited. I had watched Charlton get ahead of both Boggs and Williams before retiring them. When he fell behind 2-1 on me, I thought I would get a fastball, but as I've said, I always looked for fastballs. And if Norm located his fastball, well, it might not have mattered what I did. When Charlton fired a fastball that was low and over the middle of the plate, I jumped on the pitch and caught it perfectly, my level swing elevating at its apex. As soon as I finished my swing, I knew that ball was gone because I had hit it so superbly. I dropped my head to the right, as I always did, and trotted around the bases, with 57,126 fans screeching. I wanted to screech, too. "I remember when O'Neill hit that home run off Charlton," Showalter said. "I said to myself, 'We've got something here.' That freaking guy stuck his freaking face in there and crushed a pitch off a guy throwing about 100. He didn't back off."

I have a scrapbook of mental memories from playing on five World Series championship teams. But, even though the homer against Norm didn't happen in the World Series, it was still one of the most rewarding and satisfying moments of my career. When I think about how tough a pitcher Norm was and what the Yankees were trying to achieve at that time, it brings backs awesome memories. It was such a thrilling time for all of us in New York. The Yankees were back! After not appearing in the postseason since 1981, we had proved that we were a powerful team again. It was so invigorating to be a part of that journey, a journey that Stick had foreseen when he acquired me from the Reds. Gary Thorne was the play-by-play announcer for that game and I absolutely loved his call of my homer off Charlton: "Oh, yeah! Tie game. Paul O'Neill," he shouted. "Goodbye into the night of New York!"

I don't watch a lot of my own highlights, but if I see a replay of that homer, I will stop and watch and listen. I get chills when I hear Gary's pulsating call. After we won that game on Jim Leyritz's dramatic homer in the fifteenth inning, a bunch of cars pulled alongside our team bus as we drove to the airport. The Bronx Zoo fans were waving out of their windows and honking their horns. There was one rabid fan who kept pointing at me, pumping his fist, and showing me his version of my home-run swing. It looked pretty awesome. Man, it's a night I'll never forget.

I thought we were going to win that series and have a special 1995, especially after the way we won Game 2. But we lost the next three games and that best-of-five series, a devastating experience because we had won 25 of our last 31 games to reach the postseason. It was Mattingly's first and only postseason appearance and he was ouststanding with a .417 average, 1 homer, and 6 runs batted in. Cap had told me he wanted to get to the postseason just so he could see how he would perform on that grand stage, and his performance was phenomenal.

That end-of-the-season flight from Seattle to New York

was as depressing as any flight I've ever taken with a team. After we had the best record in the American League at 70-43 in 1994 and the season was canceled because of the work stoppage, we wanted some redemption in 1995. We were on a path to making that happen for two glorious games, but the Mariners stifled us.

How long did that series loss stay with me? Well, Nevalee, who was pregnant with our daughter, Allie, at the time, had purchased a black-and-brown outfit in Seattle. She wore it on the flight back to New York in early October. When she tried to wear it again four months later, I asked her to get rid of the clothes. They reminded me of Seattle and that aching loss, and I didn't need any extra reminders. (I know...it's not my wife's fault, but still...I was angry with the baseball gods for that series.)

That ending was difficult on and off the field because I knew Donnie's back issues would surely cause him to retire (and he eventually did). Showalter ended up leaving, too, to become manager of the Arizona Diamondbacks, an expansion team who would debut in 1998. Stick, my great ally, departed from the general manager position and took another job in the organization. But Stick and Buck had accomplished so much in the span of a few years. They had taken a ninety-loss team and built a tough and successful one, a turnaround that set up the dynastic run that would produce four championships in five seasons.

I have long been proud to have arrived in 1993 and be a part of that process, although Mattingly stunned me when he credited me for helping spearhead the revival. "I think he should be remembered in an unbelievable manner," said Mattingly. "I think he's the guy who was the main guy in turning it around. He was a great player, but the other thing is he wouldn't settle. There was no acceptance. Nothing was good enough."

Mattingly made those comments to a reporter and then he repeated them at a Yankees dinner, and I got goose bumps. I've stressed how much I respected Donnie and how we were hitting buddies and close friends. What he said about my impact was one of the greatest compliments I've ever received. When I was in the middle of playing a season, I never stopped to think how I might be influencing my teammates. I just wanted to work hard, hit line drives, and be someone who helped a club win. For Donnie to say I was a catalyst for a resounding change, that resonated with me.

I had won a World Series with the Reds in 1990 and we were competitive every year, so I knew what it was like to win and to try to win. But when I was traded to New York, I learned just how much owner George Steinbrenner and the rest of the organization despised losing. It wasn't accepted. I came to the Yankees during a transitional period, so it was an opportune time to arrive and try to have an impact.

And when the 1996 season began, there was a new player in pinstripes who would have as enormous an impact as any player could.

———— ∽ ————

The first time Derek Jeter played for the Yankees was May 29, 1995. He went 0 for 5 against the Mariners in Seattle. A humble start, for sure. After the game, Derek and his father couldn't find any place for a late meal so they ended up eating at McDonald's.

Yes, fairy-tale journeys sometimes include a pit stop for a Big Mac and fries.

The next night, Jeter slapped a single to left field off Tim Belcher for his first major-league hit, which launched him to about 3,500 more. In Jeter's first stint, he only stayed with the team for about two weeks before returning to the minors. Oh, by the way, Jeter and Mariano Rivera were both sent down to Triple-A on the same day. They shared the emotions and the disappointment of that day and vowed they would both be back and become indispensable Yankees.

They were right. They were beyond right.

Even though Jeter was a twenty-year-old kid when he made his debut with the Yankees and was twenty-one when he opened the 1996 season as our starting shortstop, I always thought he carried himself with unbelievable confidence. Jeter was the Yankees' first-round draft pick from 1992 and the can't-miss prospect. But do you know what? Some of those can't-miss prospects do miss. So, I watched Jeter with a lot of curiosity and a lot of hope. We were a talented team with championship aspirations and we needed him to succeed. Jeter has spoken about not being afraid to fail and that showed in the way he performed.

I spent two decades in professional dugouts where I talked to and observed my teammates, and there were numerous times when a player was 0 for 4 and he wasn't interested in getting that fifth at bat. Some players would say, "It's already been an awful day. I'm not going to make it worse by wishing for another at bat. I will just take my 0 for 4 and go home." From the outset, I noticed that Derek wasn't like that. We could be up 10-1 or down 10-1. If he was 0 for 4, he wanted that extra at bat. He wanted to hit. He loved to hit, but more importantly, he believed in his ability to hit. That's not always true with every player.

Once I got the opportunity to see Jeter prepare every day and hit every day, I loved his approach. Derek stayed with his plan and was loyal to what he wanted to do: his desire was to stay inside the ball and hit it to right field or right-center. He was still a skinny kid of about 175 pounds, so I figured he'd eventually produce some power, but that was never going to be his calling card. In fact, from the first time I studied Jeter as a hitter, his approach never changed. He was as good at using that inside-out swing as anyone I've ever seen.

When I reflect on who Jeter became for the Yankees, I think about how fellow shortstops Alex Rodriguez and Nomar Garciaparra were thriving at the same time. It's admirable that Derek never tried to change to match what those players did. Both A-Rod and Nomar had more power than Derek, but Derek—whose career high in homers was 24—just kept doing what he did best. He would swing early in the count because he was aggressive, he would slash singles and doubles to the right side, and he would produce in crucial situations. Sometimes, a hitter's ego can get in the way and he can develop bad habits because he's trying to do something other hitters do. Derek never did that.

Because Jeter used that inside-out swing and stayed inside

the ball, he was never afraid of getting jammed with pitches, so he didn't fly open and take an off-balance swing. By doing that, Jeter's bat stayed in the zone longer and allowed him to put more balls in play. If the pitcher made a mistake with an off-speed pitch, Derek would be able to pull the baseball. One problem for a pull-conscious hitter is when he thinks about pulling the ball before it's ever released, a mistake that can lead to a lot of futile at bats. The pitcher will dictate where a batter hits the ball based on where he locates the pitch, so the hitter who decides how he's going to swing before the pitch is even thrown is being reckless. Again, I never saw Derek plagued by that issue because he let the ball travel and he wasn't trying to pull the ball.

In terms of making pitchers uncomfortable, Jeter was a perfect player to have leading off or hitting second, because he was always in attack mode. Jeter wasn't the type to have technical conversations about hitting, like Mattingly or Boggs, because he preferred to keep things simple. If Jeter saw a first-pitch fastball that he could smash, he would swing. He wasn't looking to work a walk or have an extended at bat. He could and he would—if that's how the at bat unfolded. But he was ready to do damage from pitch one.

It took a lot of faith for Jeter to hit in the way that he did. He trusted himself and his instincts even more than he trusted scouting reports. For Jeter, the approach was to "see the ball, hit the ball." Derek told me he didn't want to clutter his mind with too much information about the pitcher's tendencies. And, again, that's about having faith in himself. When I watched Derek, his approach worked for him and it was genius in its simplicity. It's the kind of advice a coach would give to a Little Leaguer: See the ball. Hit the ball.

Anyone who watched me play knows that I was intense. I barked at the umpires. I threw my bat and my helmet. I didn't treat water or Gatorade coolers kindly. I snapped at umpires some more. I admit that I was an intense, passionate hothead.

Do you know who was also intense? Jeter.

Actually, I think Jeter's intensity and his I-am-going-to-destroy-you attitude haven't been highlighted enough. Since Jeter was the matinee idol in New York and was so beloved by the Yankee fans and respected by his teammates and his opponents, there's a perception that Jeter was a cuddly sort who was just out on the field to have a fun time.

Do I think Jeter had fun playing the game? Yes.

Do I think Jeter wanted to dominate the opponent? Absolutely.

Jeter became friends with Michael Jordan after they initially spoke at an Arizona Fall League game in 1994 and Jeter had that same kind of confidence as Michael. While it was easier for everyone to see in Michael's mannerisms and the way he trash-talked opponents, I saw some of that extreme confidence in Derek, too. Basically, he would show you why he was better than you. That intensity, whether people detected it or not, was a huge part of his success.

Jeter's intensity was evident in the simple yet impactful way he sprinted ninety feet to first base in every at bat of his career. We're all supposed to do that, right? But not every player does. I didn't. I was guilty of being frustrated and putting my head down and jogging to first. Not Jeter. He was so intent on beating the opposition that he was trying to force the defense to make that play a bit quicker, even if it was a tapper back to the mound. He was putting the pressure on the other team and setting an example for his team.

On certain days, Torre thought we should take a mental or physical break and he would cancel batting practice. That always created a dilemma for me, Jeter, and Tino Martinez. We hated taking days off. We loved to hit. We would be restless as we sat by our lockers and we'd nominate one of us to pester Torre into letting us hit. Quite often, it was Jeter who walked into Torre's office and requested that we be allowed to take our normal pregame swings. Joe would usually acquiesce and tell the team that hitting was optional, which would make me, Derek, and Tino much happier.

That is a behind-the-scenes example of how much Jeter loved to work and prepare. He didn't show up, put on a Yankees uniform, and turn into Superman. He was a really hard worker, a really talented athlete, and a really intense player. "Different people have different keys on how to do things," Torre said. "Derek Jeter had a fire in his stomach and it was as hot as anybody else's."

Still, I understand why there was a belief that Jeter was Mister Nice Guy, because, well, he was a nice guy on the field. I found it mind-boggling that Jeter was able to talk to fans while he was in the on-deck circle. Are you kidding me? How did his mind allow him to be so casual before an at bat? I used to ask him, "How can you do a magazine photo shoot in the morning, then do some interviews in the clubhouse in the afternoon, and then talk to fans before you're about to hit, and then be locked-in by the time you made it to the plate?" Jeter would shrug and say that he was able to lock in to the at bat in the time that it took him to walk from the on-deck circle to the batter's box. Trust me, that's some Hall-of-Fame focus right there.

From the moment I woke up, I was thinking about my at bats in that day's game. If anything distracted me, I couldn't handle it. Mentally, I just wasn't as strong as Derek in being able to flip that switch and morph from having a chat in the on-deck circle to focus on the next two-seam fastball. I would never think of talking to fans from the on-deck circle, because that was a distraction I didn't need. I have heard numerous players say that we can't just flip on a switch to play baseball. I agreed with that until I played with Jeter. He was so talented and so focused that I think he was able to flip on a switch.

We're all wired differently, and Jeter's self-confidence was something that helped him stand above me—and honestly, above most players. If Jeter had a poor game and went 0 for 5, he would almost skip out of the clubhouse while eating an ice-cream cone and shouting, "Sato!" That was his nickname for Jorge Posada, and it was his not-so-subtle reminder to Jorge to move quicker so they could leave.

Why did Jeter seem so carefree? Because he was confident. He believed he would have a much better game the next day.

In my ever-racing mind, if I didn't get any hits today, I was worried I wouldn't get any hits the next day. I wasn't eating an ice-cream cone after an 0 for 5. I was more likely to throw a gallon of ice cream against the wall. The fact that Jeter had that kind of mentality at such a young age was impressive. Really impressive.

When you're a young player, it's natural to let one horrible swing in your first at bat overtake you and influence the rest of your game. I had to learn to adjust my swing and reboot my mind and not let an entire game get away from me because I popped out on a hittable fastball in the first inning. If you're a young player and you worry that every at bat determines whether you'll play tomorrow, it's hard to have patience and hard not to press. Jeter didn't press.

To conquer the potential chaos of a draining day at the Stadium, I had a routine of sitting quietly by my locker for a few minutes before games. I didn't meditate or read, but I did think about the opposing pitcher and what I wanted to do. My locker was on the back wall of the clubhouse, between the trainer's room and the lounge, a spot where players steadily drifted past me as they got ready for the game.

Jeter's locker was on the adjacent wall to my right, about forty feet from mine. But during the 1997 season, I felt as if Jeter was about four feet away from me. Since I was scalding the baseball and hitting .340 in July, Jeter would stop every time he passed by my locker. And every time he stopped, he would say the same thing: "O'Neill," Jeter would bellow, "you can hit!" And then he'd smile or smack me on the back or put his hands on his hips and wait for me to mutter a response. But Derek did this *every day*. Sometimes, I would respond by saying, "Yeah, Jete, I can really hit," or tell him to be quiet and wave him away like it was a joke.

But I must admit, I liked the playful banter, I liked the praise, and I eventually looked forward to Jeter's daily visit. Everyone likes compliments, but there was something special about the dynamic player who was becoming the face of our franchise telling me I could hit. I had played over a thousand more games in the majors than Derek had at that point, but it was meaningful for such a fearless and confident hitter to make a ritual of giving me some props.

As I've said, hitters hear voices all the time. The hitter needs to determine what he wants to absorb and what he wants to ignore. All Jeter did was tell me that he liked the way I was swinging the bat. But because it was Jeter and because he did it with style, it resonated with me. Even today, I can still hear him saying it. It's a forever connection. It also makes me want to pick up a bat and crush a few doubles, so I can hear Jeter say it one more time.

CHAPTER 4

I Was Never as Zen as Bernie Williams

I'm wearing my Yankees uniform and sitting by my locker because I'm getting ready for a game at the Stadium, but I can't get my socks on my feet. That's weird. Why won't my socks fit?

"Now batting for the Yankees..."

Is this some kind of joke? I always pull up my socks before I slip my legs into my pants or button my jersey. But I just stared down for the tenth time and my socks are wrestling with my feet and the socks are winning. The rest of my uniform is all set. But I'm panicking because I can't get these socks over my ankles.

"The right fielder, number twenty-one..."

Slow down! Someone tell Bob Sheppard to stop announcing me. I'm not ready to hit. If I can't wear these socks, I can't put on my spikes. If I can't put on my spikes, I can't hit. Can someone please tell him not to announce my name?

"PAUL O'NEILL. Number twenty-one."

Oh, no. He's already announced me and I'm still in the clubhouse with my bare feet. I looked everywhere for another pair of socks. I looked inside a few shoe boxes, I looked inside my spikes, I looked in my pockets and on my clothes hangers (even though I've never hung socks on a hanger). I even searched in other players' lockers. But my search was in vain. I can't use these socks.

"Now batting for the Yankees..."

Stop announcing me as the next batter! Please turn off the public address system until I solve this sock saga. Also, why is the clubhouse empty? I need help, but there's no one here. No teammates, no clubhouse attendants, and no bat boys. Maybe Mr. Sheppard can make an announcement about someone helping me with these slippery socks. I have to hit. I can't do that in naked feet. Please, someone help. This feels like a nightmare and I need it to end.

And then I'd wake up, because it *was* a nightmare, a recurring nightmare. The nightmare of the uncooperative socks happened at least twice a year: before spring training and before Opening Day. I didn't need a dream expert to tell me why I was having this dream. Here's a hint: it wasn't about the socks.

I dreamt about the socks and about potentially missing an at bat because I was always fearful about not being prepared for tomorrow. It's as simple as that. As I went to bed each night, I reviewed what I needed to do to be ready for the next game, the next pitcher, and the next opponent. If you're thinking about something before you go to sleep, there's a good chance you'll dream about it. And that's what happened with me. Over and over.

That dream was a microcosm of how I acted as a player—I played with intensity and I was obsessive about being prepared. When I told my teammates about the dream, they laughed because they could envision me screaming and hollering for help with my socks. I did a lot of screaming and hollering during my career, so no one should be surprised by me doing that in a dream, too. That's who I was—that's who I've always been. That's what helped make me the passionate player I was. And the complete opposite of my soft-spoken, stoic, always zen teammate Bernie Williams.

Bernie was so cool and so chill, and he never seemed to let games frustrate him. Over a thousand times, I watched Bernie stroll out of the clubhouse after a game, and a bystander wouldn't have been able to tell if he cracked a game-winning homer or if he dropped a fly ball to lose the game. Staying placid and even-keeled worked for Bernie because that's the way he was wired and that was his personality. I was a bit different.

If something or someone irritated me or if I flopped in a critical at bat, I would react. Immediately and powerfully. I treated Gatorade coolers and water coolers like punching bags. I flung my helmet so much that it had scuff marks. I slammed my bats so viciously into walls that they splintered. I whipped my batting gloves into the stands (because they had to be the reason I made an out, right?). I yelled at myself and, of course, I yelled at umpires. I didn't know how to be calm on the field.

Standing in right field and mulling over an 0 for 4, there were numerous nights I knew I probably wasn't going to sleep when I got home. If I didn't get a hit in my next bat, I would spend most of the night staring at the ceiling. That was motivation for me. I wanted to do well. There were times when I heard fans booing after a lousy performance, but that wasn't really what motivated me. I motivated myself. You want to get better and you want to do it for yourself. Work harder! Be better! Derek Jeter, who was the master at looking forward, could leave the ballpark and forget about what just happened across the last few hours. I couldn't really do that. I would live with myself all night and treat losses like burdens.

Baseball isn't an easy game, even for the best players. It's a really hard game to play, and it's even harder to thrive at, as I did professionally for two decades. Even when I became a regular starting player and won a World Series ring with the 1990 Reds and a second ring with the 1996 Yankees (and then won three more with the Yankees in 1998, 1999, and 2000), I never stopped appreciating how tough it was to succeed as a baseball player. And the only way for me to survive in that environment was to play as if I were one hideous game away from losing my job and losing everything.

As I dug into the batter's box to face the next pitcher, I always knew my batting average, my homers, and my runs batted in were being displayed somewhere on the scoreboard. Most of the time, I didn't stare at those numbers, numbers that I already knew. But when those big, bold numbers were flashing before the eyes of 40,000 people, the pressure percolated inside of me. Those numbers are your life. That's who you are. That's how you're doing every day. That's your self-worth. Calling those stats my self-worth probably wasn't the most self-assured approach to take into an at bat, but that's the power I gave to those numbers. And that's why I exhibited some rage if a strike call went against me or if I took a lame swing. If my stats weren't where I wanted them to be, they would haunt and taunt me.

"Paul didn't play at his best when he was real comfortable," said Buck Showalter, my former Yankees manager who now manages the Mets. "I liked him when he had a little freaking edge. He was so much more of a team player and cared about winning more than people really knew."

My fiery personality was born and developed in a big backyard on East Cooke Road in Columbus, Ohio, which was framed by maple and apple trees and filled with four older brothers who called me "the baby." My brothers, who ranged in age from two to eight years older than me, didn't want "the baby" to interfere with their sports activities. I had to beg and whine and be a nuisance to get my way. Sound like anyone you saw playing right field for the Yankees?

But that backyard ended up being a vital testing ground for me, because when I finally got the chance to join them as a five-year-old, I had to prove myself. If I didn't show my brothers I could at least be a decent little player, they would have ignored me and kicked me out of the game. I was constantly trying to prove myself, constantly pushing myself. And when I lost to them, I was a sore loser. "That might have something to do with how I act now," I once told a reporter. "I don't want to get inside my head about it. I might not like what I see."

Half seriously and half jokingly, I used to say my biggest mistake as a major leaguer was a failure to save my on-the-field eruptions until I was out of camera range. If I had waited until I had vanished from the camera's view, my explosions wouldn't have been seen by millions of people. But that wasn't realistic because my reactions were so immediate and raw. I couldn't wait. If I was aggravated about something, I had no patience. I wasn't the type to take a deep breath or count to ten.

Like I said, I wasn't as zen as Bernie Williams.

Because Bernie was perfectly relaxed and, at times, a little oblivious, we would often joke with him and tell him tomorrow's game was at 1:00 p.m. even though it was a 7:00 p.m. start. We always wondered if Bernie would actually check the schedule or if he would just show up six hours earlier.

If we had stretching exercises on the field at 4:20 p.m., Bernie, who was one of the fastest players on the team, would occasionally amble out of the dugout at 4:19. And he would still be buckling his belt. We would scream and shout at Bernie and tell him he was going to be fined in our kangaroo court, but none of our antics flustered him. An incredible talent and an affable man, Bernie operated best when he was in his own world. "I survived all those years in New York," Williams once said, "by staying under the radar as much as possible."

Staying under the radar was a challenge for me. Sometimes, I would see replays of what I had done, whether it was punching a cooler multiple times, rushing toward an umpire with the veins popping out of my neck, or kicking my equipment or a stack of cups, and I would ask myself, "How in the world could you do something like that?"

But as embarrassed and aghast as I could be about my own behavior, I knew why I did it. Emotion and intensity are a significant part of playing baseball. I'm convinced that I wouldn't have gotten as much out of my abilities if I was calmer and told myself that I would simply get the pitcher the next day. I wasn't wired that way. In baseball, we play virtually every day, so there's an opportunity to have a good game or a bad game and be judged every single day. And I judged myself critically.

That self-criticism and rage once caused me to use the bat that had just made an out to destroy the bathroom toilet that's behind the dugout. Teammates told me it sounded as if someone had brought a jackhammer into the bathroom. My destructive behavior led to a meeting with Joe Torre, my supportive manager, and General Manager Bob Watson. I felt like a high school student who cut class and had been summoned to the principal's office. After telling me how much he loved my passion to succeed and how he loved my serious approach to getting better, Torre also issued a stern warning: "Paulie," Torre said, "if you hurt yourself, I will break your neck. You can do all kinds of acting out, but if you hurt yourself and you can't play the next day, then I will kill you."

I understood Joe's message. Venting was acceptable. Injuring myself or my teammates wouldn't have been acceptable. I guess Joe and Bob were just trying to control my insanity, and I listened to them. I never wanted to do anything that would hurt me or anyone else and fortunately, I didn't.

"I didn't mind him doing those things as long as he didn't put himself in harm's way," Torre explained. "You never know what's going to happen when you break a bat or something. You have to let it out. It's a passionate game. I don't think there was anybody more passionate than Paul O'Neill."

Let's be honest: everyone has a little Paul O'Neill in them, a little anger, a little rage, and a little need to respond. Countless times, I would speak to Yankees fans and they would tell me how they wanted to throw their computer off their desk or slam-dunk their phone after a discouraging day at work. Basically, they wanted to do what I did. Even Torre, the most stoic manager I've ever seen, admitted he had moments when he wanted to be as animated and annoyed as me, but he had self-control. "Even though it looked like I was relaxed and laid-back in the dugout, I wasn't always relaxed," Torre said. "I held it in and didn't act out because I didn't want to be seen. And I never wanted the players to see my reaction. I couldn't do that."

As I would have expected, Joe also had that self-control as a player. But Joe conceded he had a destructive side and did something I've never done: "When I was playing and I had a bad at bat, I used to come back to the dugout and there were these metal hooks above your head where you could hang a jacket or some equipment," Torre recalled. "I would sit there and I would grab on to that hook and I'd just twist it and twist it until I pulled that hook right out of the wall. But no one saw it. I got my aggression out without anybody ever seeing."

It's always nice to be recognized and receive an award, which happened to me when the Yankees presented me with a trophy for an organizational hitting honor. The trophy featured a small figure in a batting stance and I stored it in my locker. But soon after that little man arrived, I stopped hitting. My memory is fuzzy with the numbers, so I don't remember if I was 2 for 15 or worse. But I do know that I wasn't living up to what that trophy represented. I wasn't hitting. Frustrated and annoyed, I took a bat and smashed the trophy into a bunch of pieces.

Was that reckless? Yes. But I was mad at myself and I needed to vent, and I was tired of looking at that trophy. I guess that trophy was just in the wrong place at the wrong time. At that time, there were 24 other players in the clubhouse. How many of them would have smashed a trophy like that? Maybe a handful would have thought about it. But I was the one who actually did it.

I answered hundreds of questions about my fiery approach, my intense play, and my passionate style during my career. One thought-provoking question stayed with me. When my son Andy was six years old, a reporter asked me how I would feel if Andy slammed a bat or a helmet and explained that it was OK to do that because Dad did it all the time. I said it would bother me because that meant I had not set a good example. But if Andy was angry because he didn't perform as well as he wanted to, then I would have fully supported his actions. No doubt, I would have been proud of him for taking the game seriously.

There's an exceptional website called BaseballReference.com that has every baseball statistic imaginable from the major leagues and the Negro leagues and is a must-visit for any fan. If you want to know how I did on June 3, 1994, just click on my page and navigate to my yearly game logs. For the record, I was 1 for 4 in the Yankees' 7-4 loss to the Kansas City Royals.

The site includes biographical and personal information for every player, so it lists Columbus, Ohio, as my place of birth and says I am six feet four and 200 pounds (that was my weight when I was younger because I played at 210 pounds for most of my career). The site also has these details for me: Bats: Left. Throws: Left. Kicks: Left. Kicks? I never played for the Cincinnati Bengals, but someone at the site has a clever sense of humor, because I'm the rare baseball player who also has a kicking background.

While playing right field for the Reds on July 5, 1989, I fielded a single by Philadelphia's Lenny Dykstra, and in my haste to throw the ball home to get Steve Jeltz, I bobbled the ball a few times and couldn't corral it. Then, assuming that Jeltz had already scored from second, I kicked the baseball. Yes, in my frustration over presumably allowing the winning run to score, I pulled my leg back like Jim Breech and kicked the ball. But my silly kick sailed beautifully in the air, traveled about one hundred feet, and made it accurately to first baseman Todd Benzinger. Jeltz, who didn't see my bobbles or my punt, shockingly stayed at third. "We had a scouting report on O'Neill's arm," said Phillies' manager Nick Leyva, "but not his foot."

I was embarrassed by the play—deeply embarrassed. We subsequently lost on a passed ball, but my mistake was a popular topic in postgame interviews. I didn't have much of an explanation for reporters. I said I had rushed to field the ball as fast as I could and didn't make a clean play. I promised I'd never kick a ball again. On that day, I also told my teammates I was destined to be on the blooper reel for the rest of my life. I was right. Three decades later, my kick can be found on YouTube and it still generates a lot of views (more than 550,000 and counting). It's comical to watch, because it's the type of goofy play that never happens on a baseball field. Unless I'm involved.

Fortunately, kicking a baseball was a one-time thing. But in terms of quirky habits that I had on the field, I talked to myself. A lot. This is actually something many players do. To fight my doubts and to stay mentally strong, I talked to myself before every pitch. I would whisper, "Stay on top and hit it hard. Stay on top and hit it hard." I would repeat that over and over. I would almost chant it so it became embedded in my mind.

By saying that multiple times before every pitch, my focus was on the task, and my focus was toward a positive. When I did this, I drowned out any negative thoughts that might have been creeping in about the last pitch or my last swing. But every time I said it, I also needed to visualize it and see it happening in my mind. It wasn't just the words. It was the words and what I envisioned they would soon represent.

Whispering to myself was a confidence-building act and it was part of my overall hitting routine. To be consistent, it's pivotal to have a routine as a hitter and to stay with it during hot streaks and during slumps. When some hitters are in a groove, they might relax a bit because they're feeling so good at the plate. When I was hitting well, I thought I had to work harder to maintain it. Some productive hitters might take a day off from batting practice because they are in a solid place, but I never felt that way. I wanted to keep working to stay there.

During the tough times, I would preach to myself even more. At the plate. In the dugout. In the clubhouse. I would remind myself to "stay on top and hit it hard." Once a hitter's mind wanders from his mechanics and what he must do to remain successful, he has lost his focus and he will have a difficult time avoiding the negative thoughts.

Dozens and dozens of times, I heard batters say, "You have to tip your cap to the pitcher," after an opposing pitcher had shut down a team. Dozens and dozens of times, I cringed when I heard that cliché. Not only did I hate it, I disagreed with it.

During my career, there wasn't one strike that was thrown to me that I failed to connect with for a hit at some point. I don't care if it was a two-seam fastball that tailed toward the outside corner, a slider that dived below my hands, or a four-seam fastball up in the zone. Whatever type of pitch it was, I had smacked that pitch for a hit during a game. That's why I grew aggravated with the notion of tipping my cap to indicate that the pitcher had been so flawless. Don't tell me to tip my cap! I had hit that pitch before, and this time, I made an out. I never thought the pitcher got me out. I always thought I had made the out. Again, that goes back to the whole idea of being in control of the at bat.

For Bernie, my mild-mannered buddy, being in control meant eliminating any distractions. During the 2002 season, I was announcing games and I noticed Williams, the most musically inclined player in the majors, didn't have a walk-up song. On May 5, he asked the Yankees' scoreboard team not to play music during his at bats. Williams hit 2 homers against Seattle in that game, and after that, he continued walking to the plate to the sounds of silence. "It just got a little distracting," Bernie said. "Sometimes, it would be too much. I didn't want to hear anything anymore."

While Bernie was on his way to winning an American League batting title with a .339 average in 1998, David Cone, our teammate, asked him what he thought of while he was in the batter's box. "Nothing," Bernie said, which was a perfect answer and a perfectly suitable answer from Bernie. The fewer thoughts a hitter has, the more focused he will be.

I marveled at Bernie's talent as a center fielder who had 2,336 hits, 287 homers, a .297 average, and an .858 OPS, and who also won four World Series titles, four Gold Glove Awards, and made five All-Star teams. I also marveled at Bernie's talent as a classical guitarist who has been nominated for a Latin Grammy Award. How many people dream of being a major leaguer? And how many dream of being an accomplished musician? Tens of millions dream about both of those premium vocations. And Bernie, my super talented teammate, has flourished in both careers. He's had two dream jobs. Amazing.

I took drum lessons as a kid and enjoyed playing them, but sports were my priority, and that meant putting my sticks away. When there was a work stoppage in 1994 and 1995, I was bored without baseball and I needed something to keep me occupied. That's when I picked up the sticks again and started banging on the drums all day.

Since Bernie was a skilled and serious musician who played his guitar by his locker, on the team bus, and on the team plane, we decided to form a two-man band. If players made a right-hand turn out of the clubhouse at Yankee Stadium and walked down the hallway until it ended, they would find the indoor batting cage. Adjacent to the cage was a room that was called the paint room because, well, that's where they stored the paint that was used to spruce up the aging ballpark. Amidst the dozens of paint cans in that dusty room, Bernie and I created our own music studio.

Any time we had a rain delay or we didn't have batting practice on the field, the two of us would scurry down to the paint room to jam. I was very blessed that Liberty DeVitto, the drummer for Billy Joel's band, and Mark Rivera, the saxophone player for Joel, sent me a snazzy set of drums. We set them up in the paint room and we started rocking and rolling.

One of our featured songs was Tracy Chapman's "Give Me One Reason," a bluesy love song with a tinge of defiance. Bernie loved the slow, haunting guitar riff in the tune and I liked the nuanced drumbeat that kicks in about forty-five seconds into the song. If we ever had to audition for someone, that would have been the song we played. The only thing we needed was a capable vocalist.

Besides the Chapman song, we played "Honky Tonk Women" by the Rolling Stones and "Sweet Home Alabama" by Lynyrd Skynyrd, and a few other classic-rock tunes. Bernie was a true professional, and he could play just about any song. I was the amateur in the band, and I was just trying to keep the beat, keep it strong.

Every once in a while, a VIP would visit the paint room. One day, Max Weinberg, the drummer for Bruce Springsteen's E Street Band, was at the Stadium. Excitedly, we brought him to our private sanctuary. Mighty Max slipped behind the drum kit and tried to teach me "Dancing in the Dark." Max smoothly showed me the beat, which was different than most of Springsteen's songs, and I gave it a shot. But while I'd once played "Gloria" onstage with John Cougar Mellencamp, I will be honest and admit the Bruce song sounded a lot better when Bruce's drummer played it.

Watching Bernie play the guitar was so soulful and so peaceful that it perfectly suited his calm personality. Bernie plucked away at the strings, coolly moving from one chord to the next. And then there was me behind the drums, banging away like a man possessed and trying to keep up with the beat. Yeah, I'd say that manic approach fit my personality, too.

When Bernie and I weren't making part-time music, we were often batting back-to-back on a full-time basis in the Yankee lineup. As a switch-hitter who had power, Williams was a menace for pitchers and for managers who tried to match up against him. With Bernie looming behind me, it was a comfortable place for me because I knew I'd get a lot of good pitches to hit.

During our fabulous 1998 season, both Bernie and I experienced a power outage at the outset of the season. In early May, we were both still searching for our first homer. I didn't consider myself a home-run hitter, but no homers in the first five weeks of the season was pathetic. We were the only two players who had hit at least 20 homers in 1997 who hadn't yet homered in 1998. As a playful way to conquer the drought, Bernie and I agreed to bet one dollar on who would hit the first homer.

With one overdue swing on May 3, I finally clubbed a homer off Tim Belcher, a pitcher whom I had performed well against (23 for 76, .303 average, and 7 homers) in my career. It was also my 200th homer, and it was such a relief to go deep. I actually homered in three straight games and finished the season with 24 homers and 116 runs batted in. Bernie, who smacked his first homer on May 12, had 26 homers and 97 RBIs. We both rebounded very nicely from those early goose eggs. However, I think my teammate and bandmate still owes me a buck.

Believe it or not, I wanted to have cordial relationships with the umpires. I'm serious about that. I was ornery and outspoken, but I didn't relish the idea of arguing about pitches. I really wanted those relationships with umps to be pleasant. But with my combustible personality and quick-trigger temper, the relationships were usually more combative. Going into a game, I knew there were certain umpires who were bound to create some issues with the way they called balls and strikes. Conversely, there were also some umpires I trusted because they weren't looking to stick it to a player.

When I debuted with the Reds in 1985, I was nervous around the umpires and didn't try to say much to them. I wasn't allowed to say much. The umps didn't want to hear one word from a young hitter. But once I became more established as a player, I could ask about a pitch and at least get a short dialogue going.

Because I moaned and groaned to the umpires, I've often had people ask me if my reputation with the umps hurt me. My antics could have hurt me, but I actually think being chatty with umpires can also help a hitter. There were times I complained about a call in one at bat and then got that same borderline call to go my way in my next time up. Dealing with umpires is the same as dealing with people in our everyday lives. You're going to get along with some of them and you're not going to get along with some of them. And when it was an umpire I clashed with, I wanted to avoid two-strike situations, because I didn't want the bat taken out of my hands.

Consistency and honesty. That's all I wanted from the umpires. I didn't want to be their buddy as a way to push for extra calls. I just wanted a consistent strike zone and an honest approach. These days, umpires are evaluated more than ever. After games, the umps receive an assessment of their performance, which could include being told they miscalled several pitches on the outside corner against right-handed batters. With that evaluation system, the belief is the strike zone should be more consistent.

Respect. Umpires always want it from the players. I believed in respecting the umps, but I felt that respect needed to be a two-way street. Cone, the wise pitcher, and I have often talked about how umps need to be the calming voice, not the aggressor.

If the umpire makes a poor call, intentionally or unintentionally, he will still be on the field and working the next day. If a player goes 0 for 5 and a couple of those at bats were influenced by shabby calls, he might get sent down to the minor leagues the next day. This is a player's job and a player's life, so this is more than just a game. If a player gets emotional during a game, he should be allowed to voice his displeasure without the umpires getting too combative and turning it into a prolonged argument. When I believed something was taken away from me, like a pitch, I couldn't deal with it. It would eat away at me. That's why I would respond. Like Coney, I think the umpires should be the ones who stay cool and don't incite a player. They don't go home that night tagged with a win or a loss as the players do.

I remember an at bat where an umpire called me out on a pitch that was at least a foot outside. I'm not exaggerating. It was an awful call. I argued with the ump, but that never changes anything. As I ran out to the outfield the next day, he stopped me and said, "I'm sorry. I missed that pitch last night." I was dumbfounded. What could I say to that? Now you're telling me you missed a pitch? I respected the ump for admitting a mistake, and nodded and said "Thanks." But I still remembered him looking at me with a smug face the night before and telling me the pitch was on the corner for a strike. That type of exchange infuriated me.

In the first month of the 1998 season, I was forced to answer some questions about a book that had been written by Durwood Merrill, an active umpire. In the book *You're Out and You're Ugly, Too*, he called me the "number one whiner" and said I would be a member of his "all-complaining team." While Durwood was welcome to his opinion about me, I was surprised he was allowed to write that book as someone who was still umpiring games. If he had retired, so be it. But here was an umpire who had called me a whiner and complainer, who was still calling balls and strikes against me. That wasn't cool to me. I wonder how baseball officials would have reacted if an active player had written a book with his critiques of current umpires.

Feel free to call me a whiner or a crybaby, as some did, for arguing about balls and strikes. That's fine. When I was crying or whining, I was fighting for something very important and very valuable. I was fighting for myself, for my team, and for the chance to win a game.

Every out matters in a game, so I was incensed if I ever gave an out away and I was even more incensed if an out was taken away from us. I fouled a ball off my right foot and it dribbled to first base while we were playing the Expos on June 5, 2000. To me, the call was a no-brainer. The ball hit my foot in the batter's box, which meant it should have been a dead ball and my at bat should have continued. But inexplicably, Rich Rieker, the plate ump, ruled the ball didn't strike my foot and called me out on a grounder. I vigorously complained to Rieker and to Jim Joyce, the crew chief. But I didn't get any satisfaction with my argument. After the game, with dried blood caked behind my cracked toenail and a bloody sock in my hand, I made two predictions: "I'm going to lose my big toenail," I said. And, "I'm going to send it to him."

Guess what? I was right about both predictions. It took a few weeks for my toenail to fall off. I admit this is gross, but when the nail fell off, I packaged it inside an envelope and asked one of our clubhouse attendants to deliver it to the umpires' room at Yankee Stadium. I didn't include a note with the toenail, but I did ask our clubby to tell the umps exactly what it was. It wasn't the most sanitary action or the friendliest gesture, but I wanted to prove I was right. I have no idea if they ever received the envelope.

No one wants to be remembered for losing or for something they did during a loss. If you didn't do enough to win, nothing else matters, right? Well, not always. To some fans, I'm vividly remembered for one play, a play that came in the Yankees' loss to Cleveland in the 1997 American League Division Series. And George Steinbrenner is a big reason why I'm remembered for it, because that's when he dubbed me "the Warrior."

I already mentioned the two-out double I lined off José Mesa in the ninth inning of Game 5. The ball narrowly missed being a homer, and I had to sprawl and tumble and dive my way into second base to secure a double. We lost the game on the next at bat, but that awkward slide led to Mr. Steinbrenner lavishing praise on me. "He showed you do not give up. Ever. Ever," Steinbrenner told *The New York Times*. "A heart of a lion—that's what you think of when you think of Paul O'Neill. I wish I had 25 like him. He's the ultimate warrior."

After the loss, Mr. Steinbrenner shook my hand and congratulated me for my superb series (.421 average, 2 homers, and 7 RBIs), but I told him it didn't matter because we had lost. But Mr. Steinbrenner persisted, and also told reporters, "What does that say for Paul O'Neill? That he's the ultimate warrior. In my mind, that play at second base was his signature moment."

That was a monumental compliment from the boss. But while I was still playing, I would get embarrassed by the nickname because I didn't feel comfortable with that label. I played hard all the time. I didn't think I needed a nickname to validate what I did on the field. However, that name followed me.

After Derek Jeter became Mr. November and hit a game-winning homer to power us past the Arizona Diamondbacks—4-3 in ten innings in Game 4 of the 2001 World Series—I tried to be inconspicuous and use a side entrance to return to the clubhouse. That's when Mr. Steinbrenner noticed me, hustled over, hugged me, and shouted, "The Warrior! Here's the Warrior!" The boss was thrilled with our improbable win, which had been fueled by Tino Martinez's homer in the ninth to tie the game, so Mr. Steinbrenner poked me in the chest as he announced my nickname. I didn't want that attention. I never did. Mr. Steinbrenner's actions caused reporters to descend upon us, but I wasn't about to allow this to become a scene. I shook my head and said, "Don't start with that stuff again. Don't you start." And then I slipped away into the clubhouse.

It took a while for me to grow comfortable with being called "the Warrior," but as the years passed, I appreciated the magnitude and the meaning of what Mr. Steinbrenner said. For George Steinbrenner, a ferocious competitor whose sole focus was on winning, to give me a nickname that symbolized the essence of trying to win, that was wonderful. In retirement, I have embraced the name. I had better. When I broadcast games at Yankee Stadium for the YES Network, they often play "The Warrior" by Scandal. I stand and wave to the fans and I think about Mr. Steinbrenner and a lot of fond memories. "George Steinbrenner named Paul right," Torre said. "He called him the warrior. He just never stopped trying and he was always there for us."

In retrospect, being called "the Warrior" was infinitely better than being called chubby. While Mr. Steinbrenner never called me that, he was disappointed when I arrived for one spring training at 220 pounds. I had difficulty maintaining my weight during the course of a grueling season. To combat that, I bulked up in the off-season and was in the best shape of my life at 220. But that was 10 pounds over my listed weight, meaning I was required to retreat to a back field in Fort Lauderdale, Florida, and run laps at a place the players called "the Farm." Of course, there were a few other *f*-words that players used to describe the farm when they were sent there. Some of my heftier teammates laughed at my presence on the field because I clearly wasn't overweight. But the scale said what the scale said, so I abided by Mr. Steinbrenner's rules and ran in the blazing sun to lose the weight. That was an LOL moment before anyone even knew what *LOL* meant.

There are so many things I miss about playing in the major leagues. I miss the hyperventilating, hyperactive fans. I miss the one-on-one duels with the pitcher. I miss the camaraderie of competing and hanging out with my teammates. And I miss playing postseason games. Every October, as the weather gets chillier and the skies get darker a little earlier, I think about some amazing playoff memories.

But there's also one big thing I don't miss. I don't miss my panicky sock dream that was really a panicky nightmare.

Once I retired in 2001, I rarely dreamed about any ill-fitting socks again. I sleep soundly before spring training and before Opening Day. I haven't had that dream in a long time, so I must be totally prepared for tomorrow now.

I guess you could call that personal growth.

———◦◦———

CHAPTER 5

I Like Homers, but I Like DJ LeMahieu More

Five days into my major-league career with the Reds, I was being the dutiful and quiet rookie and doing exactly what Pete Rose, my manager and teammate, had recommended I do: watching how my teammates were preparing and performing and trying to learn from them. I barely spoke in my early days in the dugout because I knew I was as much a student as I was a player in September 1985. Listen and learn.

Before the ninth inning of a lopsided game at Wrigley Field, class was definitely in session for me. Dave Parker, our hulking right fielder and a man who just seemed way bigger and way better than everyone else in baseball, sat beside me and made a bold prediction. If Parker got an at bat in the ninth, he said, "I'm taking this guy deep."

This "guy" was the Cubs' Lee Smith, who was one of the best closers in the big leagues, and who would eventually be inducted into the Hall of Fame. I couldn't believe how self-assured Parker sounded when he forecast hitting a homer against Smith. He said it with such conviction. It wasn't false bravado. It was all confidence, almost as if he had visualized the at bat and had already seen the result. I was mesmerized by Parker's prediction.

Sure enough, we loaded the bases on a couple of hits and a walk and advanced to Parker's spot in the lineup. A few minutes earlier, Parker had enough faith, optimism, and swagger to basically tell a new major leaguer, "Watch this, kid. This is how it's done." And he did it. Parker smashed Smith's fastball for a grand slam, leaving me in shock. We lost to the Cubs 9-7, but that was secondary to me. All I remembered was how Dave Parker was a bad dude and a hitting hero. "I hope he catches Cobb before me," joked Rose, who was three hits away from eclipsing Ty Cobb's hit record.

I knew how supremely talented Parker was and how he had won a Most Valuable Player Award, two batting titles, and a few Gold Gloves, and had powered the Pittsburgh Pirates to the 1979 World Series title. But when a player accurately predicts he will do something that dramatic and that profound, it's appropriate to put that player on a pedestal and place the pedestal on top of a skyscraper. I was on the same team as Parker and I was in the same league as him, but as a twenty-two-year-old, I couldn't imagine being as imposing and intimidating as him. He had a cannon for an arm, he looked like a tight end, and he raked like a batting champion. How could I ever match that?

When I watch current hitters and the approaches some of

them take at the plate, I reflect on my experience with Parker. Parker talked about hitting a homer because he knew who he was as a hitter, and because he knew it was a possibility against one of Smith's fastballs. He didn't stroll to the plate and try to hit a homer in every at bat like an all-or-nothing hitter. He was a complete hitter who could hit the ball to all fields as he batted .290 with 2,712 hits, 339 homers, and 1,493 runs batted in during his exceptional career. As Ted Williams told me and so many other hitters: know who you are. Parker knew who he was.

These days, some hitters don't know who they are. When I say that, I don't mean everyone. But I've noticed enough of a trend, where some hitters are taking what I refer to as "home-run swings." These players are using significant uppercuts to swing at the ball and are trying to lift the ball into the seats. That has become a very popular approach for a legion of hitters in what has become known as the launch angle era. Those types of swings will produce homers, but they will also produce their share of infield pop-ups, harmless fly balls, and swings and misses.

And here's my two cents: not everyone is or should be that kind of hitter.

Let me pause to praise some of the sensational hitters who know what kind of hitters they are and who make me stop and stare at them on TV. I love watching the approaches and the exploits of Mookie Betts, Mike Trout, Juan Soto, Shohei Ohtani, Vladimir Guerrero Jr., Freddie Freeman, Aaron Judge, Ronald Acuña Jr., Fernando Tatís Jr., and many other elite players.

I've flourished and I've failed as a hitter, so I know how difficult it is to succeed in the major leagues. Ted Williams called hitting a round ball with a round bat the most difficult thing to do in sports, and I agree with him. But in that difficult pursuit, not every hitter follows Williams's advice of being focused on who they are and what they do well.

In the current version of Major League Baseball, it's a power-hungry world and a power-happy world. Home runs are the most desired commodity. It's visible in the way players try to pummel the ball into the next zip code, it's obvious in the way power hitters are rightfully rewarded with handsome salaries, and it's also apparent in the way fans react every time a ball travels 450 feet. Many batters are swinging at the bottom of the baseball to try and get the ball in the air and, more importantly, to send it sailing over the fence. My strategy was to hit on top of the baseball because I believed that gave me the best chance to make contact and hit line drives.

"It's a lot easier to hit the top of the ball than the bottom of the ball," said Buck Showalter, my former Yankees manager and the current manager of the Mets. "A guy who hits on top of the ball doesn't want to strike out. Paul tried to hit through the ball. He never hit to the ball. He hit through the ball. He'd never start out swinging up at the ball. There was too much margin for error to do that."

I know the game has changed. I understand and respect that, and I'd never denigrate how many outstanding hitters have worked so hard to become the hitters they are. I don't always love this swing-for-the-fences game in which batters bash a lot of homers (each team averaged a record-setting 1.39 homers per game in 2019) and also strike out a lot (each team averaged a record-setting 8.81 strikeouts per game in 2019). But I know how talented players must be to even have the chance to take one swing in a big-league game. And hitting a baseball is hard and getting harder.

With so many pitchers throwing close to 100 miles per hour, and with batters facing three or four different arms per game, it's never been so challenging to hit at the major-league level.

My hitting language is similar to that of many current players, because I believe in the importance of hitting the ball hard, hitting through the ball, and hitting it in the air in the form of line drives. But I think we differ in some of the methods we would use to accomplish those goals.

Like me, Kris Bryant grew up with a father who idolized Ted Williams. Mike Bryant actually received some hitting guidance from the "Splendid Splinter" when he was a minor leaguer with the Boston Red Sox in the 1980s. Imagine that good fortune. Mike was definitely blessed to receive tutorials from Williams. I received one call from Ted to talk hitting, and I was floored by our conversation and how he helped me.

According to *The New York Times*, Williams gave Mike two pieces of advice, telling him, "We're going to hit it hard and we're going to hit it in the air." Mike tutored his son on those same rules. Kris hit 26 homers and won the Rookie of the Year award for the Cubs in 2015. He clubbed 39 homers, won a Most Valuable Player Award, and helped the Cubs end an interminable 108-year drought by winning the World Series in 2016. Kris has a beautiful swing and says he tries to hit the ball in the air every time he is at the plate. Same here. Again, I was trying to hit liners.

I'm one former major leaguer with one voice, and I don't force my opinions on any hitters. Every team has hitting coaches, and players also consult their own hitting experts and hitting gurus. But any time hitters have asked me questions, I remind them there's value in grasping what kind of hitter you are and being great at being that kind of hitter. Again, that was Williams's advice: don't try to become something you're not.

If you're a line-drive hitter like me, hit line drives. If you're an opposite-field hitter like Derek Jeter, hit the ball the other way. If you're a hitter with a lot of speed like Carl Crawford, put the ball in play and use your legs. If you're a power hitter like Judge or Giancarlo Stanton, then load up and crush the ball. But here's the caveat with that last sentence: Judge and Stanton are powerful hitters who can fail to square up pitches and still be strong enough to hit them for homers. So, that puts them in rare company. I was a good major-league hitter and I couldn't do that.

I hit 281 homers in my career. I wish I had hit 581, but power hitting wasn't my strength. I would have been a much less productive hitter, in my mind, if I ever tried to consistently belt homers. I wasn't Alex Rodriguez or Ken Griffey Jr., who had gorgeous swings and also happened to be home-run hitters.

When I competed against A-Rod, I had always heard he was obsessed with hitting and loved to discuss the finer points of the craft. During his first season with the Yankees in 2004, I discovered how true that was as he spotted me by the batting cage and peppered me with questions. We were rivals and never talked hitting during my playing career, but A-Rod wanted to know my thought process when I was batting in critical situations. He was arguably the best player in baseball at that point and maybe one of the top ten players of all time, but he acted like a reporter who was writing a story about different theories on hitting. I could tell how genuinely curious he was and how he absorbed everything I said. That first conversation led to about a dozen more, and it was evident that Alex loved dissecting the art of hitting. I'm still flattered that he consulted me, because that meant he believed I knew a thing or two about hitting. "I've always been a big fan of Paul O'Neill," said Rodriguez. "When you think about situational hitting and the big moments and hitting against great pitching, it's check, check, check with him. I just always thought he went about it the right way."

When A-Rod described himself as a hitter, he said he always wanted to be a good hitter with power and not just a power hitter. With 3,115 hits and 696 homers, A-Rod obviously was a great hitter and a powerful hitter. But I understand what he meant about being a great hitter who also happened to hit for power.

Growing up in Miami, A-Rod's favorite player was Keith Hernandez, a sweet-swinging lefty and batting champion who hit line drives and hit the ball to all fields. Alex said Hernandez's approach "sung to me as a young fan who was trying to learn about the right way to hit." Like A-Rod, I could watch Hernandez swing a bat all day and all night because I connected with his approach. "If you looked at O'Neill's swings before he stepped in the box, it was always about having that top hand over the ball," Rodriguez said. "He exaggerated it so much in his pre—at bat swings because he wanted to hit on top of the ball. Paul did that as well as anybody. I think O'Neill was just a pure hitter.

"But," A-Rod continued, "his magic was in his makeup and in his grit and in his resilience. It wasn't in, 'Can he hit a ball a thousand feet?' That wasn't the magic of Paul O'Neill. The reason why he's a five-time World Champion is because of the grit inside of him. I think that's the headline and not just that he was a natural, pure hitter because he was that as well."

While Alex and I were different hitters because I was a left-handed hitter who hit liners to all fields and he was a right-handed hitter who was one of the greatest home-run hitters of his generation, we did have some similarities, too. Alex is six feet three, and I'm an inch taller, and we both had leg kicks, so discussing that timing mechanism fueled many of our chats. "Paul was always asking me how I was feeling and whether I was close to where I wanted to be," A-Rod said. "Because of our size and our leg kicks, we talked about seeing the ball and getting our foot down on time and all the different routines we had. He just loved to talk hitting. And I loved talking hitting with him."

Every time I broadcast Yankees games for the YES Network, I analyze the hitters and try to decipher their plans and uncover what they're attempting to do at the plate. As much as we all love to see prodigious homers by the herculean Judge and Stanton, the hitter I most enjoy watching and the hitter I most identify with is DJ LeMahieu.

Why? Because LeMahieu hits the ball to every inch of the ballpark, he puts the ball in play, and he isn't trying to hit moon shots in every at bat. To me, it's refreshing to see because that's the way I used to hit. "Paul is similar to DJ," Showalter said. "But, really, the right way to say that is that DJ is similar to Paul."

In this era of defensive shifts, when teams are moving their infielders all over the field to strategize against a hitter's tendencies, LeMahieu is the ultimate all-fields hitter. In DJ's three years with the Yankees, he's seen one defensive shift. Just one! That's remarkable. And when the Blue Jays shifted against DJ while Santiago Espinal, a position player, was pitching the ninth inning of a laugher on September 15, 2020, LeMahieu slugged a homer. He remained immune to any shift.

Some batters are predictable, and that allows teams to shift against them in almost every at bat. Joey Gallo, a left-handed pull hitter, always sees more fielders loaded on the right side of the diamond. Like many of today's hitters, Gallo doesn't try to beat the shift by rapping a single to left. He has said he tries to conquer the shift by hitting the ball over it.

And there are a lot of shifts to conquer. During the 2021 season, the 30 teams combined to shift a staggering 55,595 times, according to BaseballSavant.com. The website noted that the Dodgers and the Mets shifted on over 50 percent of the plate appearances while they were on defense. As recently as 2016, only two teams shifted more than 25 percent of the time.

Using spray charts that show where a player is most likely to hit the ball, teams position their fielders accordingly. It's fascinating how prominent shifting has become as teams attempt to neutralize hitters. I remember Andy Pettitte, my Yankees teammate, studying spray charts in the 1990s to gauge hitters' tendencies and then deciding how he would pitch them. If Andy noticed that a right-handed batter was a pull hitter and never hit the ball to the right side, he would toss pitches on the outside corner to generate some weak contact or some uncomfortable swings.

Shifts can swallow up many hits and frustrate hitters. But when I hear hitters say they can't hit the ball the other way to beat the shift, I disagree. I used the whole field, so hitting the ball the opposite way wasn't foreign to me. When hitters argue that it's difficult to do that, I say, "Well, it's the major leagues. Everything is difficult about being a major-league hitter."

This is a hard game and it moves fast, but I think hitters can use an inside-out swing to be able to go the opposite way. With an inside-out swing, my hands stayed close to my body and the barrel of the bat remained behind my hands until my swing moved into the hitting zone. As soon as my bat was in that zone, I would push the barrel forward to make contact. I had to wait longer on the pitch when I swung like this, but it was also the easiest way to stroke a hit to the opposite field. It takes some practice and some commitment to use an inside-out swing, but it can be done, and it can be a very effective way to hit.

However, here's what has happened with the mentality of today's game. If a left-handed slugger fights a pitch off and bloops it into left for a single, or if he pushes a bunt to the empty left side for a single, I'm sure he stands on first base and wonders, "Did I do enough damage in that at bat? If I fouled that pitch off or didn't swing at it, would I have gotten a pitch that I could have hit out of the ballpark?" Nowadays, that's just where the thought process is in the game.

That type of second-guessing as a hitter will always exist. Even when I played, I might try and drag a bunt for a hit because the second baseman was playing so deep. And after I did that, I'd wonder if I really could have hit the ball into the gap. As a hitter, I understand the desire to want to do more. And there's nothing that makes more of a statement than a home run.

Every time I mention how much I enjoy contact hitting and how much I abhor strikeouts, some people misunderstand me and construe that as an anti-homer stance. I must stress that I love homers, too. What hitter doesn't love homers? What I dislike is how some hitters sell out to bash homers and how that creates an avalanche of swings and misses. But homers are frequently the greatest tonic for any offense. The Atlanta Braves out-homered the Houston Astros 11-2 to win the 2021 World Series in six games. Of the 25 runs the Braves scored, 18 came via the homer.

Still, as electrifying as homers are, there are times when hitting a homer isn't the only solution in a game. Here's why: If my team is trailing by 5 runs and I lead off with a homer, we're still behind by 4. But if I lace a single and we get the pitcher into the stretch position, that could make him uncomfortable and more vulnerable. Manager Joe Torre used to call it getting to the pitcher and putting "a chip in his armor." And that base runner might lead to a situation where our opponents have to tax their bullpen. Maybe the innocent single is the start of a rally that ends up being more productive than one solo homer.

And that's one of the reasons I'm fond of LeMahieu's hitting. In DJ's first two seasons with the Yankees, he put up stunning numbers with a .336 batting average, a .386 on-base percentage, and a .536 slugging percentage, and twice finished in the top four in the American League MVP voting. He was as reliable as any hitter in the majors as he stung the ball solidly and sprayed hits around the ballpark. LeMahieu hit .268 with a .349 OBP and a .362 slugging percentage and struggled in 2021, but a sports hernia injury adversely impacted him. Still, if I were a manager, I would want LeMahieu (and his style) in the batter's box in any crucial situation. I wish there were more DJ clones.

"The people who say they can't hit like DJ LeMahieu, my question to them would be, 'Have you tried?'" Showalter said. "DJ LeMahieu has no ego when it comes to hitting. You can tell he's happy to hit a single up the middle. You can tell he's happy when he blocks one off and gets a hit between first and second." I agree with Buck. And I was the same way as DJ—I hated it when I didn't put the ball in play, but to put the ball in play, a player needs to have a certain approach and can't always be thinking about going yard.

We've conditioned a generation of batters to understand the importance of their launch angle and their exit velocity, which are valuable terms that tell hitters a lot about the way they are swinging the bat. These days, teenagers take swings at batting facilities and instantly know how many miles per hour they pounded the baseball. I'm not sure that's always a positive development, because I would rather see the kid focusing on the different elements of his swing. Incidentally, once the uppercut swing and the pursuit of launch angle became so popular, pitchers also became shrewder about attacking hitters. They feature more four-seam fastballs up in the zone because those are more challenging to hit when a batter is swinging up at the ball.

In addition to launch angle and exit velocity, I think we should also emphasize the importance of plate coverage and being able to connect with pitches that are in the strike zone or close to the zone. While we didn't specifically know a batter's contact rate percentage when I played, I knew which hitters were skillful at putting the ball in play. I didn't need the stats to identify those hitters because they stood out to me. Nowadays, I'm always interested in that statistic when I'm broadcasting because that percentage tells me which players are the tougher outs and don't swing and miss as much.

"A lot of the guys in today's game, they don't have great range with the bat," Showalter said. "You want to see hitters who have the range to cover different pitches and make good, hard contact. Paul had great range with the bat. So did Don Mattingly. So did Wade Boggs. They didn't waste at bats and they put the ball in play.

"Do you know where the great range comes from?" Showalter continued. "It comes from not trying to hit the ball out of the ballpark. DJ LeMahieu has great range with the bat, but again, that's from not chasing balls that you can't get. There are so many hitters today who are just chasing the home run. It's not their fault. They're being compensated for it. I don't blame the players. I don't blame the kids. It's the people who are teaching it and rewarding it. Those are the guys I blame."

For selfish reasons, I've always hoped that a contact hitter like LeMahieu would be the catalyst who enticed teams into having more balanced lineups. The LeMahieu I watched during 2019 and 2020 is the type of versatile and productive batter who could have played on our great Yankees teams of the 1990s, because he would have been able to get on base, drive in runs, and keep the offensive line moving. And keeping that line moving with multiple hits in a row has become tougher because of the lack of balls in play. From 2001, my last season, until 2019, strikeouts in baseball rose 24 percent.

In this era of so many swings and misses, even my contact-hitting hero sometimes misses pitches—LeMahieu struck out ninety-four times in 679 plate appearances in 2021. Still, that's a strikeout percentage of 13.8, which is very good and was the nineteenth lowest in the major leagues. DJ's career strikeout percentage is 14.6. Mine was 14. It's evident that DJ is superb at putting the ball in play because his swings have produced contact 87 percent of the time in his career, according to Fangraphs.com. He hits the ball on the barrel of the bat and hits it very hard. He's quick enough to handle the ball that's away from him and slash it to right field. And he's still able to get to the ball that's inside on him and do damage with that pitch. And to me, that's the definition of a hitter.

I've been involved in numerous discussions with baseball people about the way a player swings and how he swings at a specific launch angle. But the art of hitting is being able to adjust when you're beat by a pitch and bringing your hands in to make contact. That allows a hitter to stay through the ball and for his bat to be out ahead a little bit so he's not rolling over the ball and hitting a weak grounder. If a batter has a swing that creates a specific launch angle and that's the way he hits all the time, how can he adjust to a pitch that's moving or a pitch that isn't where he thought it was going to be coming out of the pitcher's hand? That's a really tough assignment for any hitter and is one of the reasons we see so many strikeouts.

Call me a curmudgeon or accuse me of being old-school, but I prefer a balanced lineup, not an everyone-swing-for-a-homer lineup. If I were devising a lineup, I would want a couple of speedy contact hitters who average .300 and got on base a lot at the top. I would want some power hitters in the middle, and I would want some players who put the ball in play at the bottom. Keep the pressure on the pitcher!

And I guarantee that balanced lineup would be very tough on pitchers. There's always a way to score some runs with that sort of lineup, and yes, some of them would be via the long ball. But some of the runs would also come from moving runners over, from hitting sacrifice flies, from taking extra bases, and from playing strong fundamental baseball. I like a versatile lineup better than a lineup that's so reliant on power, because there will be some nights when you don't have any power and then you don't have any offense. Several pitchers have told me they preferred going after the one-dimensional hitters.

"I hated facing the guys who were trying to put the ball in play and who didn't want to strike out," said Al Leiter, who pitched for the Mets, the Yankees, the Blue Jays, and the Marlins and won 162 games in his career. "I enjoyed facing the guys with the bigger swings who were trying to hit the ball out of the yard because they had more holes in their swings.

They were easier for me than a guy like Tony Gwynn or Paul O'Neill."

Then Leiter added, "I think it's shameful in so many ways that you get a guy who is batting .225 or .230 and strikes out 150 or 160 times a year and he thinks he's doing his job because he hit 32 homers. I would love to face a guy like that. He won't walk because he doesn't have a recognition of the strike zone. He's got a lot of swing and miss in his game, he doesn't try to put the ball in play or go the other way. Man, it would be a field day to face guys like that."

If I were playing today, what kind of hitter would I be? I'm asked that question a lot. My answer is simple and boring: I would stay loyal to who I was and I would still try to stay on top of the ball and hit line drives around the entire field. I don't think I would have altered my swing to search for more homers just because so many other players were doing it.

As I've detailed, I was pressured to try that with the Reds and I considered myself a failure for hitting a career-high 28 homers in 1991, because I also batted .256 with 107 strikeouts. Sure, I hit some extra homers, but I always believed I was a better hitter when I was hitting the ball the other way and driving in runs. After I was traded to the Yankees and didn't have to worry about pulling the ball anymore, and could share hitting philosophies with Mattingly and Boggs, I was relieved. That's why I think I would be the same hitter in 2022 as I was in 1994, 1998, or 2001. With the way hitting has evolved, Leiter isn't so sure about that.

"I know Paul is saying that as a guy who played a long time and had a very good career," Leiter said. "I think you end up being a product of your environment and your surroundings at the time. My guess is Paul would be equally good if he was playing right now. My guess is there would be some pressure and influence based on all of the data from the technology they now have and that would probably even convince a guy like Paul that, 'Hey, while you average twenty homers a year, we think that we can get you closer to thirty a year by doing this.' Depending on where a player was in his career, I'm not sure if he'd do that and if he'd allow that change to his approach."

I respect Al's opinion, but the data would have needed to be overwhelming for me to ever adjust the line-drive approach my father instilled in me. Once again, a hitter is going to hear a variety of voices throughout his career. It's important for a hitter to know who he is as a hitter and trust certain voices and dismiss the others. I believed in that philosophy, and that's why I'm confident I wouldn't have changed.

"Paul was a talented commodity that you didn't want to mess up," Showalter said. "You knew how much he could achieve if you didn't mess him up. You could have someone who would over-coach him. With today's methods, someone would try to over-coach him. And Paul would ask, 'Why do you want me to do it that way?' Paul wouldn't just blindly accept a certain way they wanted him to do it. He would say, 'This pitcher is throwing ninety-four with a good breaking ball. So why am I supposed to do it your way?' Paul was probably a lot smarter than most of his hitting coaches."

Joe Torre, my other former Yankees manager, also agreed that I wouldn't have made any changes: "Paul's approach and his style would play today," Torre said. "Paul O'Neill had his own way of doing things. He knew what worked for him and he knew what he had to do."

With the major leagues' average fastball velocity at 95 miles per hour, an all-time high, and batters trying to be quick to catch up with these pitches, I've noticed some hitters using a questionable strategy. If a pitcher throws exceptionally hard, some hitters are trying to match that forcefulness with long, aggressive swings. That's a careless approach. In their minds, batters can't process being quick to the ball without trying to do too much with that swing, and that results in a long swing and that makes them slow to the ball.

When I faced Nolan Ryan, I would swing harder and that was a mistake. The harder a batter swings, the longer his swing is, the more he drags the bat, and the slower his bat is. If a batter trusts he can get to the ball, doesn't worry about getting jammed, and doesn't take a vicious (and long) swing, his swing will be quicker to the ball. Of course, I learned this lesson too late since I was 0 for 10 with five strikeouts against Ryan. To be honest, I'm not sure this adjustment would have worked against Ryan. I heard the baseball whizzing by me more than I saw the baseball against Ryan.

Over and over, I've mentioned how I always wanted to put the ball in play and how I was embarrassed with strikeouts. When I was a younger hitter with the Reds, I actually wanted to make contact before I got to two strikes because I'd get panicky about being in a two-strike situation. As I became a more experienced hitter, I didn't mind hitting with two strikes. I considered it a challenge and I was confident in myself and my ability to make contact. Naturally, I didn't relish being in 0-2 and 1-2 counts against the nastiest pitchers because they had deceptive swing-and-miss pitches—and if they made their pitch, I would be wandering back to the dugout.

With two strikes, I would put myself in a less aggressive mode in terms of trying to drive the ball. Once a batter has two strikes, he has already missed some chances. However he missed those pitches, whether it was a foul ball, a called strike, or a swing and miss, those two strikes were his opportunities to unleash that big swing. That pitch that the batter wanted to smash for a big shot? That chance is gone and now he must adjust. Like I said, I would take a more controlled swing and shoot for the middle of the field in two-strike situations.

Pete Rose became baseball's all-time hit king, and he was also one of the kings of a two-strike approach. Do you know why? Because Pete had a two-strike approach from the first pitch of the at bat. His mission was to put the ball in play, so while he was an aggressive hitter, he was smart aggressive, not reckless aggressive. Even Pete's assertive body language and his crouching stance told the pitcher that it was going to be a chore to retire him on an 0-0 pitch or an 0-2 pitch.

When I observe some of today's hitters, I don't see enough adjustments being made with two strikes. Instead, I see a lot of hitters who are still taking their home-run swing with two strikes, and while that will surely lead to some deep flies, it will also lead to more strikeouts. Hitting the ball hard was my mission, but simply putting the ball in play was a part of that mission. Again, I know the high velocity of pitchers and the parade of relievers being used in every game means hitting is arduous, but strikeouts exasperate me. There's a reason they have nicknames like golden sombrero for four strikeouts. If there's a negative nickname for something, it's best to avoid doing it.

One future Hall of Famer who has forever impressed me with his approach, including with two strikes, is Miguel Cabrera. With two-strike counts, Cabrera has shown he is talented enough and smart enough to turn right-center field into a target. Because Cabrera has so much strength, he can shoot the ball the opposite way and those shots can turn into homers. That's an example of a shrewd and powerful hitter who knows exactly what he's doing against certain pitches.

On every pitch, I wanted to be in the same position when the ball zoomed into the hitting area because, by doing that, I gave myself a chance to connect with any pitch. If a hitter has closed off his hip or has opened his front side too quickly or is late with his leg kick, he won't be in the same spot every time. And to me, having all those parts of my body moving seamlessly and consistently was essential to being a potent hitter. It's the equivalent of a pitcher repeating his delivery on every pitch.

As far as my swing was concerned, I have stressed how I wanted to stay on top of the ball, stay through the ball, and hit the ball hard. As I tried to stay on top of the ball, my bat would be level as it traveled through the zone. As I continued my swing, my bat would follow through over my shoulder and into a slight uppercut. In *The Science of Hitting*, Ted Williams wrote, "A slight upswing is the best," because it matches the trajectory of the incoming pitch, increasing the area of solid contact.

However a batter decides to swing, he should do what makes him the most comfortable. I had a lightbulb moment and became a much better and smarter hitter when I understood how to get extension on the inside part of the baseball. As a left-handed hitter, that would be the right side of the ball as I was looking at it out of the pitcher's hand. This was a gradual process, and I can't pinpoint the precise moment it happened, but it was early in my Yankees career.

When most batters talk about hitting inside the baseball, they are thinking about using a chicken-wing approach, where they flail their elbows like a scrappy chicken to fight a pitch off and stay alive in an at bat. That's a survival swing, not a powerful swing. But if a hitter truly learns to extend and hit through the ball on the inside path and really drive it, that's nirvana.

The best way I can describe this hitting technique is to view the baseball as a heavier spherical object, like a shot-put. The batter wants to hit the inside part of the shot and continue that swing forcefully and drive through it. If the batter stops swinging aggressively once he makes contact with the ball, he loses a lot of his power. That extension through the ball is the key to really driving the ball.

When a batter comes around the ball and hits the outside part of the ball, he will usually end up hooking that ball and hitting it foul. As a hitter, you need to hunt for that mistake pitch that is right down the middle and learn how to hit it on the inside part and extend, I mean really extend through it, and trust me, that ball will carry forever.

To get that extension, I would keep my body locked-in on inside pitches and I wouldn't be fearful of getting jammed. I was trying to swing and get extension through the ball by hitting it right back toward the pitcher, an approach that kept me focused on hitting the ball from gap to gap. And that approach also kept me from pulling off the ball and hitting it feebly. By executing my swing in this way, I wouldn't lose any power and the ball would explode off my bat. When I perfected this wrinkle in hitting, it was eye-opening. There was a renewed sense of comfort, and it felt like I had the answers to the test before I had even taken the test. I knew I was the best hitter I could be.

How did I eventually make this important adjustment? Like any improvement in hitting, it was because of repetition and the maturity that came with more at bats. For a good chunk of my career, the idea of hitting the ball on the inside meant I was flicking it away in an emergency swing to simply get to another pitch. As soon as I learned how to get extension, to have a powerful swing through the inside of the ball, and to stay on the top of the ball, man, that made me so much more confident and productive.

———◦◦———

As someone who hit on top of the baseball and who visualized doing that, my bat would level out through the zone and advance into a slight uppercut, and ideally, I would hit a rocket of a line drive. That was always my goal. Conversely, there are a lot of current hitters who want to hit under the ball and who want to launch fly balls. That wasn't my swing and that approach wouldn't have worked for me. Hitting under the ball wouldn't have been comfortable for me and wouldn't have helped what I was trying to accomplish at the plate.

Strikeouts, walks, and home runs are the three true outcomes in baseball, and we see a lot of them in the majors these days. In fact, more than 35 percent of all plate appearances ended in a strikeout, a walk, or a homer in 2019 through 2021. And as enthralling as homers and strikeouts—and maybe a pivotal walk (see Armando Benítez)—can be, even baseball's decision makers have admitted that the sport needs more action and that the pace of play needs to improve.

Before the 2021 season, Major League Baseball instituted some experimental rules in conjunction with various levels of the minor leagues. The changes included a limit on defensive shifting, a fifteen-second pitch clock, robotic umpires, slightly larger bases, and a cap on a pitcher's pick-off attempts. There's no guarantee any of these rules will ever be adopted at the major-league level. But, since baseball officials are studying them, there is a chance we will see one or more of them added.

The rule that intrigues me the most was a crackdown on shifting at the Double-A level, as all four infielders had to have their feet on the back portion of the infield dirt as the pitch was delivered. The infielders couldn't have a heel or a toe on the outfield grass, so there were no Double-A second basemen positioned in shallow right field to swipe potential hits from lefty pull hitters.

As much as I have said consistent shifting wouldn't have bothered me, I like this rule change and I hope it gets implemented in the big leagues. I think it's needed. The average major-league batting average was .270 in 2000, but the proliferation of shifting and the powerful arms throwing tic-tacs caused the average to plummet to .244 in 2021.

The first time an infielder shifted against me was when José Lind, the Gold Glove second baseman for the Pirates, positioned himself in short right field. I can still see the slick-fielding Lind sliding across the AstroTurf to field a hard grounder that would have been a single and throwing me out at first. I thought about countering Lind's placement by dragging a bunt toward second because it would have easily been a hit. But I never tried that, which was an oversight. Still, if teams had shifted against me as regularly as they shift now, I would have adjusted and hit the ball the other way. "Would they shift on Paul if he was playing today?" Showalter said. "If they decided to shift, Paul would have blistered a shift. He would have taken his ego out of it. He would have taken his three hits to left field, right through the shortstop hole. If you think about DJ LeMahieu, it's the same way. They can't shift against him."

If this rule on limiting shifts becomes part of the majors in some form, perhaps the game will again feature batters hitting the ball where it's pitched and hitting behind the runners and hitting a certain way in certain counts. Ask any pitcher. The lineup with some balance and some versatility can be a tougher lineup for them to tame. "I would rather face the guys with the big, looping swings who were trying to go deep," said David Cone, my former Yankees teammate. "The guys who gave me the most trouble were the guys who were just trying to put the ball in play and hit line drives."

I think the game of baseball always evolves and always

adapts, and there's also a copycat element to the sport. When a team does something a bit differently and it's successful, the other teams will soon imitate them. We've seen that with the way teams shift on defense, the aggressive way they use their relievers in games, and the way they use openers as starting pitchers.

When we won a World Series title with the 1990 Reds, we had Randy Myers, Norm Charlton, and Rob Dibble as "the Nasty Boys" in our bullpen. All three of them were late-inning terminators, and they'd enter games and shut our opponents down. The trio combined to allow one run in 24 1/3 innings in the 1990 postseason. As much as Oakland's Tony La Russa was a master at employing his relievers situationally, I don't think there had ever been a team that used three pitchers as deftly and as dominantly as Manager Lou Piniella used Myers, Charlton, and Dibble that season. I think Lou was ahead of his time.

And what happened? Other teams noticed, and the bullpen became much more vital than it had ever been. And as I watch baseball these days, I wonder if the game might eventually shift toward a more contact-oriented offense. Nothing will ever be as crucial as homers for immediate impact and immediate offense, but there are other ways for teams to score runs when homers are absent.

I'm biased because contact mattered to me as a player, and it still matters to me as a retired player who loves the sport. I think strikeouts throttle an offense, but that philosophy mostly doesn't exist today. When a team has eight or nine players who all try to go deep, there will be some epic nights of offensive joy. But, when those power hitters fizzle, there will be some frustrating nights with lots of swings and misses.

In my crystal ball that peers at baseball's future, I can see a team modifying its offensive approach and fielding a lineup that blends more LeMahieu-type hitters with some power hitters. And I see that team eventually winning a championship. And I see other teams mimicking that approach and favoring more contact hitters. I really hope my crystal ball is accurate because I hate seeing all these strikeouts. Always have and always will.

———— ⊃○⊂ ————

CHAPTER 6

Facing Randy Johnson—
Wish Me Luck

He was tall, menacing, and intimidating—a six-foot-ten pitcher who reveled in being the villain on the mound. And Randy Johnson was a superb villain. He looked the part, with scraggly brown hair that dropped to his shoulders and a sinister mustache and soul patch. And more importantly, he pumped 100-mile-per-hour fastballs and knee-bending sliders past batters.

I was one of those batters—one of those helpless batters.

When I describe Johnson as a villain, I should note that he was only a villain to the opposing team. He was a lean and lanky superhero to his team because of the way he flustered talented major leaguers and generated a succession of wayward swings.

As a left-handed hitter, trying to connect against the left-handed Johnson was one of the most torturous experiences of my career. I was somewhat fortunate in that I didn't face him much—I went 0 for 5 with three strikeouts. But during those at bats, I knew what it was like to feel overmatched. If I put the bat on the ball against him, even if it was a foul ball, I considered that an accomplishment.

There were several reasons Johnson was difficult for me to hit, but his release point was a major factor in unnerving me. When Johnson uncorked a pitch from a low, three-quarter arm angle, it looked like he was slinging the ball at me from near the second baseman. That's how far Johnson was situated toward the first-base side of the rubber and how much his arm stretched toward first. In addition, Johnson's long stride toward the batter allowed his arm to be about ten feet closer to the plate. When he finally released the pitch, it was coming from about fifty feet, not sixty feet and six inches.

Good luck with that.

Typically, I would tell myself not to commit too early against a left-hander and to keep my front shoulder closed to my body because that would allow me to be quick to the ball as I tried to hit outside pitches. But because of Johnson's release point, I had to open up my front shoulder and start my swing early, or I would have little chance of catching up with any of his pitches. Once I opened up, I had given him the outside part of the plate. So, that was my dilemma against Johnson: If I didn't open up and start my swing early, I wouldn't be able to hit anything. If I did open up and start my swing early, I would sacrifice anything on the outside part of the plate. I called Johnson a villain for a reason. My at bats were like something out of a horror movie and Johnson prevailed in every scene.

Some of those scenes occurred during the 1995 American League Division Series between the Yankees and the Mariners. That series was exciting, dramatic, and ultimately depressing because we lost to the Mariners 6-5 in eleven innings in Game 5. We carried a one-run lead into the bottom of the eleventh, but Edgar Martínez smoked a two-run double into the left-field corner off Jack McDowell to catapult the Mariners to the win.

With the score tied 4-4 in the ninth, Lou Piniella, my old Reds manager who was now managing the Mariners, pushed all his chips into the middle of the table when he summoned Johnson from the bullpen. Johnson had pitched seven innings and thrown 117 pitches two days earlier, but we had two men on and were threatening to take the lead.

As "Welcome to the Jungle" by Guns N' Roses blared at the Kingdome, Johnson walked in from the left-field bullpen like a pro wrestler who was poised to annihilate every man in the ring. He didn't run. He walked. He took his time, wiping his brow, adjusting his cap, and tugging at his belt. Johnson proceeded to strike out Wade Boggs, retire Bernie Williams on an infield pop-out, and got me to wave at a slider and pop out to the catcher. Welcome to the jungle, indeed.

After Randy Velarde's run-scoring single gave us a 5-4 lead in the top of the eleventh, I had an unforgettable encounter with Johnson. Piniella had instructed Johnson to intentionally walk Williams and put two runners on base for me. If I were Lou, I would have done the same thing. At that point in Bernie's career, the switch-hitter was 10 for 30 (.333 average) off Johnson.

While I waited near the batter's box, I took a deep breath and rubbed my right eye, my dominant eye. I reminded myself to stay relaxed, to stay on top of the ball, and to not open my front shoulder too soon. I knew I had to start my swing early, but I didn't want to go too soon or I wouldn't have a chance. I began my swing on time, took a solid cut, and connected with a slider. Boom! Well, it wasn't really a boom. I fouled the pitch off. "Damn," I thought, "that was a pitch I could have slugged." Apparently, Johnson felt the same way because he flashed a smile at me. I considered his smile a message: you had your pitch.

I took a second slider for a ball before swinging and missing on a fastball that was down the middle. I had no shot at that pitch. I fouled off an inside fastball with another swing that was more about self-protection than actually trying to smack a hit. On the fifth pitch, I was fooled on a slider and lunged to foul it off. Before the next pitch, Chris Widger, the catcher, met with Johnson because they apparently couldn't agree on what to throw. I adjusted my helmet and anxiously waited. Johnson went back to another fastball and located it perfectly on the outside corner for a called strike three. Remember how I said I couldn't get to outside pitches if I opened up my shoulder too soon? That's precisely what happened. Johnson knew my weakness against him and exploited it.

I was miserable about striking out and leaving two runners on base. I was even more miserable when we lost that game by one run and that misery lasted for months. But do you know what it is kind of strange to admit? I remember that at bat as a cool moment in my career because of Johnson's smile. For a future Hall of Famer and one of the most imposing pitchers of my generation to acknowledge me in that way was meaningful. I think Johnson smiled because a hitter he respected had taken a good swing and had barely missed a pitch. This might be the only futile at bat in my career that I actually discuss with a half smirk and a half smile on my face. I despised the result, but I enjoyed the skirmish.

I guess it was to be expected that I would struggle against Johnson, who had 303 victories, won four Cy Young Awards, struck out 4,875 batters—second all-time to Nolan Ryan's 5,714—and who made an army of lefty hitters look foolish. But how can I explain my endless troubles against Jesse Orosco? I was 1 for 18 with five strikeouts against this smart lefty. It wasn't Orosco's velocity that throttled me because he didn't throw particularly hard. Mostly, it was about his release point, too.

Orosco stood on the first-base side of the rubber and released his pitches a little above his shoulder so he was also kind of slinging the ball at batters. And Orosco had a great breaking pitch that he called a curveball. Sometimes, it looked like a slider to me and I couldn't pick it up. Unlike Johnson, it wasn't about intimidation with Orosco. It was about frustration. I should have been able to get some hits against Orosco, but it was difficult to connect when I wasn't seeing the baseball out of his hand. Every time I faced Jesse, I felt like it was 0-2 before the at bat even started.

"I tried to use the breaking ball to sweep away from him," said Orosco. "When he swung, he had a swing that could cover the low part of the strike zone. But I really didn't want to pitch him up in the zone. I used to see if I could get some strikes with the breaking pitch to get ahead and then get him to go after the ball that was down.

"I know there were at bats where I would throw a fastball that was low and on the outside corner and it was called a strike and Paul would look at me," he continued, with a laugh. "And Paul wouldn't even look at the umpire. He would look at me. From sixty feet away, he would almost whisper, 'Was that a strike?' Well, what was I going to say?"

There was nothing for Jesse to say except, "I got you again." He was a savvy and tireless pitcher who appeared in 1,252 games, more than any pitcher in history, and he also pitched until he was forty-six years old. He used his guile against me in a game between the Orioles and the Yankees on September 17, 1995. With the bases loaded and one out in the ninth inning, the Orioles had a 2-0 lead, so they called upon Orosco to oppose me. Of course, they did! I worked the count to 3-1 before Orosco threw a fastball that I thought was low, but Umpire Richie Garcia called it a strike. Orosco then jammed me with a 3-2 fastball and I smacked into a game-ending double play. "It's a situation you put yourself in as a little kid," I said, after the game. "You don't hit into double plays when you're at home dreaming about it."

That at bat was a reminder of why Orosco was such a deceptive pitcher. I had been victimized by so many of Orosco's curves that, with a 3-2 count, I expected him to throw his swing-and-miss pitch. That hunch contradicted my approach of always being prepared for a fastball, but Orosco's mastery over me meant he had also crawled inside my head. When

Orosco's fastball veered in on me, I wasn't ready for it and I was doomed. If I had stuck with my plan and looked for a fastball, I wouldn't have been leaning over the plate as much and I might have been able to adjust and not hit the ball so weakly. Walking off the field, I asked Chris Hoiles, the Orioles' catcher, if the 3-1 pitch was a ball. He told me it was, which was useless and painful information for me to digest.

"I thought Paul was a very good ballplayer," Orosco said. "In my situation, lefties against lefties, the pitcher has the advantage. Right on right, I think the batter can see the ball differently. When it's left on left, it's tougher because they don't see lefties every day. That's where you have to make adjustments on them and have a plan of attack."

Running some sprints before games at Camden Yards, I would see Orosco and the other Baltimore relievers sauntering across the outfield and going to the bullpen. We would often make eye contact and nod, a nod that was saying, "I will see you in the eighth inning." I had a lot of respect for Jesse. He was durable and shrewd, and he had one of the greatest glove throws in baseball history. After Orosco whiffed Marty Barrett to power the Mets to the 1986 World Series title over Boston, he was so jubilant that he flung his glove about a mile into the air (it's worth a view on YouTube).

Every time we played the Orioles, I was reminded about my awful stats against Orosco. I remember a reporter telling me I was 0 for 11 and then it expanded to 0 for 14 and then it increased to 0 for 17. The zero in the hit column never changed. It was tedious and annoying. Finally, I had one at bat in which I solved Orosco, my greatest nemesis.

I should treat April 14 as a personal anniversary of sorts because that's the day in 1999 when I finally understood what it was like to get a hit off Orosco. It was a clear and comfortable sixty-five-degree day at Yankee Stadium and we bolted to a 9-7 lead. With two runners on in the seventh, I was batting and that meant it was time for my daily date with Orosco. This time, Orosco, who used a four-seam grip on his curve, tried to throw a 1-1 fastball past me. I followed the pitch out of his hand and actually saw it. I couldn't believe how well I recognized the high pitch, hammering it to center field for a three-run homer. After all of those outs, I finally had a hit. I was so relieved. While it took eighteen tries, for once, I prevailed. The homer also pushed my career RBI total to 1,001. The fans gave me a curtain call for reaching 1,000 RBI, but maybe it should have been a curtain call for collecting a hit off the invincible Orosco.

"I kind of looked at him and smiled," Orosco said. "I nodded my head a little bit. He hit that to dead center. He got me. After getting 17 outs and then he hit a bomb like that? Maybe we came out even somehow." Sorry, Jesse. That's a sweet sentiment of yours, but we weren't even close to being even. I was 1 for 18. *One for eighteen!* You dominated that battle.

As much as I struggled against Johnson, Orosco, and some other lefties, I must emphasize that I anticipated getting at least one good pitch to hit in every at bat. Because I did! I probably had only about 20 at bats in my entire career, roughly one a year, in which I didn't get a pitch to hit. Even the greatest pitchers will give hitters something to hit, because they can't throw three perfect pitches in every at bat. And this applies to top echelon pitchers like Roger Clemens and Pedro Martínez, too. But if I got a decent pitch to square up from Roger or Pedro and I fouled it off, the likelihood of me getting another good pitch to do some damage was remote. Like the message that Johnson once sent me with his smile: "You had your pitch."

My most exasperating at bats came against pitchers like Johnson or Orosco because, even if they made a mistake, I couldn't pick up the ball quickly enough to exploit the mistake. I would stand in the batter's box and do everything I usually did to be ready. But—I hate to admit this—I would feel like I didn't have a chance. When a hitter can't see the baseball, he's lost.

That potential blind spot is something that I really had to fight during the postseason because those games are such a mental grind. For instance, if I didn't pick up the ball in my first at bat against Martínez, the worst thing I could do was say, "Oh no, that's Pedro Martínez. I'm in trouble." In my next at bat against Pedro, I had to perform all of my same routines and focus on the pitch coming out of his hand, just like I did against every other pitcher. It actually took me several years to develop that mental toughness to not be occasionally overwhelmed by who I was facing. I would combat that by whispering to myself, "Stay on top and hit it hard," meaning I would try to hit on top of the baseball and drive through it. I would say that on every pitch. If I did that on every pitch, it would smother the negative thoughts. And I would inevitably get a good pitch to hit—the key was not missing it. Especially from someone like Pedro or Roger. Especially in the postseason.

I had 8,669 plate appearances in the major leagues during

the regular season and postseason and I collected 2,190 hits, including some very important hits in the month of October. But the successful plate appearance that fans frequently want to discuss ended without a hit. It ended with a walk. And I understand the interest in it and I happily discuss it. It was as critical a walk as I've ever had.

Flash back to the 2000 postseason, and we were all singing "New York, New York" for the Subway Series between the Yankees and the Mets, the first Subway Series since the Yankees defeated the Brooklyn Dodgers in 1956. I was excited to be competing in such a monumental series and excited that the Yankees had the chance to win our third straight championship and our fourth in the last five years.

But personally, I was also in a depressing place because of the way I had been struggling. I had a right hip pointer that required a cortisone shot before the series, and I wasn't even sure I would be able to run or play against the Mets. Plus, I had managed only one extra base hit in the previous seven weeks. My timing was erratic, I couldn't catch up with pitches, and I couldn't drive the ball, either. Every hitter wants to be at his best in a World Series, but I wasn't anywhere close to my best. I was 9 for 39 (.231 average) with 5 RBIs in the first two rounds of the playoffs.

We were two outs away from losing Game 1 as I settled into the back of the batter's box against Armando Benítez, a 230-pound closer who had a fastball that nearly touched 100 miles per hour and who had struck out 35 percent of the batters he faced that season. From the first pitch, I was in survival mode against Benítez—pure survival mode. We were trailing

3-2, so I had to do anything I could to get on base and start a ninth-inning rally.

Benítez's first pitch was a low fastball that missed the strike zone. After that pitch, I stepped out of the box and took a few practice swings. That routine became a theme for the at bat. I wanted to slow Benítez down, but I also wanted to slow myself and the game down, too. Those pressure-packed moments can move very fast, but I had some control of the pacing. I needed to exert it.

I was ready for Benítez's next pitch. Or at least I thought I was. I swung through a 97-mile-per-hour flash of white. If Benítez threw that same pitch two more times, my at bat would end with a K because I didn't think I could connect against his heat. Benítez fired another fastball down the middle and I stared at it for a second strike. I was down 1-2 and I had not felt this helpless in a long time.

Get some control, I told myself, as I retreated from the box. I took a few more practice swings. The fans at Yankee Stadium were restless and pensive, waiting and hoping for something to happen. Benítez threw me that same fastball and I lunged to cover it and punched it foul, into the seats down the left-field line. That swing was the epitome of survival mode as I kind of flung the bat at the ball and made contact.

Before the fifth pitch of the at bat, Benítez shook off two signs and then pumped another fastball. Once again, I barely connected and lifted it into foul territory behind third base. Robin Ventura, the third baseman, drifted toward the seats and leapt into the second row, but he collided with some fans and wasn't able to make what would have been a phenomenal catch. Ventura's valiant effort came extremely close to ending my at bat, but I was still alive and flailing away. I have seen hitting magicians like Wade Boggs or Ichiro Suzuki intentionally hit foul balls and try to get to a certain pitch in a preferred location. That wasn't what I was doing. I was trying to put the ball in play, but I couldn't do it.

After five straight fastballs, Benítez threw a splitter that faded off the outside corner and pushed the count to 2-2. Then Benítez missed with a 96-mile-per-hour fastball to set up a full count. I spread the dirt around at the top of the batter's box with my cleats. There was no real reason for doing that, but again, it was a way of slowing me down. On the television broadcast, Tim McCarver, the analyst, said, "O'Neill has not caught up with a fastball during this at bat. Benítez has blown it right by him." McCarver was right. And then came another Benítez fastball and another soft foul ball down the left-field line.

"Defensive swings this entire at bat by Paul O'Neill," said Joe Buck, the play-by-play announcer. Buck was right, too. I shook my head, wandered around the box, and hoped I could get on base. Although I've always been told the hitter has the advantage when the at bat stretches longer, I didn't feel that way. If Benítez threw one more powerful fastball, I was going to be another strikeout victim.

The ninth pitch was a 98-mile-per-hour fastball and I stayed alive again and flicked into the seats along the left-field line. It was the fourth foul ball off Benítez, the fourth time I had managed to prolong the at bat. I licked my lips and looked toward left, trying to unearth a way to dump a hit in that direction. Did I even have enough bat speed to do that?

Staring in for his next sign, I thought Benítez looked stoic, even confident. That probably meant he was preparing to throw me another fastball. And he did. He threw a 3-2 fastball and it tailed outside for ball four, ending the ten-pitch duel. I had a walk, a precious walk. Because it had been such a long at bat, I felt like I had hit a home run when I heard the umpire say, "Ball four." If Benítez had known how lost I felt, he would have zoomed three fastballs down the middle and been done with me. It was a draining experience for both of us, but all of a sudden, we had a base runner and the start of something.

"That at bat," said Manager Joe Torre, "was miraculous."

Pinch-hitters Luis Polonia and José Vizcaíno followed with singles to load the bases, and Chuck Knoblauch's sacrifice fly tied the game, 3-3. Benítez blew the save and blew the chance to help the Mets win Game 1. Vizcaíno's two-out, bases-loaded single off Turk Wendell lifted us to a 4-3 win in twelve innings, but we gave ourselves the chance to win because of what we did in the ninth. "With Paul's hitting style, I think it was apropos that he had that at bat and he was able to do what he did," said Al Leiter, who started the game for the Mets. "Paul was capable of doing that, of fouling off pitches, and he did that. And he passed the baton to the next guy."

We still had to play many innings of inspired baseball to beat a resilient Mets team in five games, but that first game was significant. Mariano Rivera, our infallible closer, was one of many players who called my ninth-inning walk a defining moment. So did Leiter: "Hell, yeah, it changed things," he said. "I've always said, and it sounds like I'm being bitter, but that game one was huge. Knowing how George Steinbrenner was and everything else. The Yankees had everything to lose and nothing to gain playing us in that series. I think that was the message from ownership and on down. I know Joe Torre felt it." Then Al added, "If Paul doesn't get that walk there, I think the Mets are high-fiving as we're walking off the field that night."

Obviously, I remember the big hits and the big homers I had in my career. But sometimes, when a team is down to its last few outs, a walk can be critical to grabbing momentum and frustrating a pitcher. When I reflect on how we won that game, that was no ordinary walk. I kept hitting foul balls to potentially get a mistake pitch or to outlast Benítez and grab a base.

My walk against Benítez receives a lot of attention because it happened in the Subway Series, but making pitchers work and generating walks was a hallmark of our Yankee lineups on those dynastic teams from 1996 to 2001. We had so many potent hitters that free passes could eventually bury a pitcher because one of our hitters was bound to produce a run-scoring hit. There were countless instances when I was facing a left-handed reliever and I was especially desperate to get on base, even with a walk, because Bernie Williams was on deck and he crushed lefties. If I could reach base, I was thrilled because that gave me a perfect spot to watch Big Bernie do damage.

"Paul might have been the poster boy for those Yankee teams in the nineties that were so hard to pitch to," Leiter said.

"They took a lot of pitches and they passed the baton. Paul epitomized that. That's what he did. He also had the ability, because he was such a good hitter, to charge one, too. It wasn't just 'Throw one on the outer third and let him hit a lazy fly ball to center field.' He would stay on it and hit a line drive to left field."

It's very gracious of Al to say that about me, especially since I was a woeful 5 for 27 off him in the regular season and postseason. I vividly remember facing Al when he was on the Blue Jays in a game that took place on August 3, 1993. We were trailing 8-6 and had runners on second and third with two outs in the ninth inning. The Jays brought in Leiter, who had one career save, because closer Duane Ward had a sore arm. I decided to be aggressive against the young lefty, who had about 200 career innings on his résumé at that point. I swung at Leiter's first pitch and drilled a rocket...right to third baseman Ed Sprague. He snared it and tossed to first. Game over.

"You warm up, you sweat, you throw one pitch, and 'Whack!'" Al said. "Paul hit a bullet right to Sprague. And I got a save out of that." One pitch and one out. That's a nice memory for Al, right? It wasn't a blissful memory for me. I sat in the dugout for ten minutes after that out, cursing the fact that I had nothing to show for stinging the ball so hard. When I finally left the dugout, I angrily smashed the clubhouse door with my bat. Call it my second hard hit with no return.

Once I became more acquainted with pitchers and detected their tendencies against me, I would visualize how I expected my at bats to unfold. These days, players study hours of video to uncover information about pitchers. But I simply wanted to know the velocity of a pitcher's fastball and what else he had in his arsenal, from a slider to a curve to a cutter to a splitter to a change. If I studied too much about what the pitchers usually did, I felt I was adjusting to them, and I never wanted to do that. I wanted to dictate what happened in the at bat.

I usually had a good idea of how I had done against different pitchers because I remembered specific at bats and specific sequences. Anyway, here are my statistics against some outstanding pitchers: I was 22 for 61 (.361 average) with 4 homers against Dennis Martínez, who had a terrific curveball that fueled him to 245 victories. I was 10 for 28 (.357 average) against Dwight Gooden, who had an otherworldly fastball and a vicious curve, and I was 14 for 44 for a .318 average against both David Cone, the slider and splitter specialist, and Mike Mussina, a Hall of Famer. Doc, Coney, and Moose were also my teammates during our careers. But I was 3 for 20 (.150 average) against David Wells, another strike-throwing lefty who baffled me, and I was 5 for 33 (.152 average) with twelve walks and five strikeouts against Clemens. I was teammates with both Boomer and Rocket, too. And Boston be damned. I was 12 for 56 (.214 average) with twenty strikeouts against Pedro, another Hall of Famer with a dazzling array of pitches, and I was 6 for 25 (.240 average) against Curt Schilling.

Hitting stress is like compound interest, so I must explain how my statistics against pitchers would sometimes infiltrate my thought process. When I knew I had strong numbers against a pitcher, I would wonder, "When is this going to end?" That's because I assumed the pitcher would make an adjustment and figure something out about me. And if I had terrible numbers against a pitcher, I would wonder, "Is this ever going to end?" That's because I thought the pitcher had discovered a weakness and could keep subduing me. Those thoughts were part of my maddening world of doubts that come with being a hitter.

I had some doubts on August 31, 1995—doubts about whether I was going to play that day. I was 0 for my last 16, which included going 0 for 8 in the last two games started by Angels' lefties Jim Abbott and Chuck Finley. Now Brian Anderson, another lefty, was starting in the series finale. I hoped I would play, because I was 5 for 10 with 2 homers off Anderson and thought it was a good matchup for me. When I saw my name in the lineup, I was relieved.

It was eighty-three degrees for the first pitch that night, warm conditions that meant the ball would normally travel at the Stadium. And sure enough, it did. I belted Anderson's 3-2 fastball more than 400 feet and into the right-center field bleachers to give us a 3-0 lead in the first inning. One inning later, I smashed a 2-1 slider off Anderson into the runway between the right and right-center bleachers for another three-run homer. I looked awkward as I reached across the plate to get to Mike Harkey's 3-2 forkball in the fifth and still poked it into the right-field seats for another home run. Three at bats, 3 homers.

Suddenly, I felt like Superman.

Slump? What slump?

It only took three swings for me to feel like a different hitter.

Something calmed me during that game. Something

unexpected. It was a brief and upbeat conversation with the affable and lovable Bobby Murcer, a former Yankee who announced our games. Once I hit 2 homers, I heard my teammates talking about the possibility of a third homer and I didn't blink. I was calm because of Bobby. Three weeks earlier, my teammate Mike Stanley cracked 3 homers in a 10-9 win over the Indians. On the field the next day, Murcer made a prediction: "Three homers in one game," Murcer said. "You'll do that one day. I did it."

Huh? Bobby said it so matter-of-factly he made me believe that a gigantic achievement wasn't so gigantic. When I combined Stanley's accomplishment with Bobby's hopeful comment, that made me a believer in myself. So, I wasn't nervous as I pursued that third homer. When a teammate you see every day does something spectacular, there's less pressure on you to duplicate it.

Since it was only the fifth inning, I knew I would have a couple of chances to hit a fourth homer. The Angels brought in Bob Patterson, the old lefty who had stifled me throughout my career, for my fourth at bat. I laced a run-scoring single right through the middle to give me 4 hits and 8 runs batted in.

My last at bat was against Troy Percival, the hard-throwing closer who squinted in for signs from his catcher and then threw 100-mile-per-hour tic-tacs. Well, I'll be honest: I didn't like my chances against him. I struck out, but that didn't detract from what I had done on that special day. After the game, I told reporters I had never even hit three straight homers while playing Home Run Derby in my backyard as a kid, and I also told them my family was probably celebrating by

jumping around the living room. "But," I added, "you still h
to come back and forget about it."

That was always my attitude. What was next? Because I grew up competing with four older brothers, I never bragged when I did something because that meant I would have to repeat the achievement the next day. And chances are, I wouldn't be able to do it again. So, I carried that self-protective attitude into the majors. I never wanted to have to live up to what I said I might be able to do. It was just easier to talk blandly about what happened and get ready for the next day. I knew tomorrow was an unknown.

There is one distinction I had as a hitter that I will playfully brag about. It's a goofy distinction that probably puts me in baseball's Dubious Hall Of Fame. Are you ready? Don't laugh. When I faced Tim Wakefield, a knuckleball pitcher who threw that funky pitch about 95 percent of the time, I still looked for a fastball.

Say what? Yes, I did. I agonized over facing Wakefield. A few days before he was scheduled to start against us, I grew tense as I thought about trying to time his floating pitches and hitting them squarely. But as I've noted, I didn't want to ever adjust to the pitcher. I wanted to do what worked for me. So, even though the whole world knew Wakefield was throwing knuckleballs, I didn't change my plan of thinking fastball. If I made any changes, I felt those changes might disrupt me for several days. Consequently, I looked fastball and adjusted every time Wakefield threw his 65-mile-per-hour pitch.

"I have to laugh because I threw my fastball maybe five percent of the time," Wakefield said. "For him to look fastball, I mean...I saw lots of different approaches against me. I saw guys move up in the box, I saw guys move closer to the plate, I saw switch-hitters hit in the opposite direction because they didn't want to ruin their left-handed swing, which was all crazy to me. I saw it all. It was pretty entertaining."

But, truthfully, Tim, did you ever speak to a hitter who did what I did and looked fastball? "I never heard anyone say they looked fastball all the time," Wakefield said. Once Tim stopped chuckling about me hunting his rare heat, he offered a scouting report on me as a hitter, and modesty aside, I appreciate how he described me: "He fought every at bat like it was his last," Wakefield said. "That's what it looked like to me. That's what I admired the most about him. He never gave away at bats. Whether he was down 2-0 or up 3-0, he would grind out the at bat. He was a fierce competitor. He was passionate about being the best he could be. For me, pitching against him was a challenge. There are some guys who stepped in there and I figured I pretty much had control of them. But for O'Neill? No, I didn't feel that way. That definitely wasn't an easy at bat for me when I had to pitch against him."

My crazy approach against Wakefield was productive, as I was 9 for 24 (.375 average) with 2 homers off him. There was only one time, one solitary moment, in which he threw me a hittable fastball. And I was ready for it. My eyes bulged and I lined it to left-center field for a double. Wakefield barely remembered it. "I might have been behind in the count with a base open," he said, "and I just tried to throw a four-seamer away from him and hoped he wouldn't hit it."

A day later, I was running sprints in the outfield when Joe

Kerrigan, the Red Sox pitching coach, approached me with a bemused look on his face. "How in the world did he throw you a fastball?" Kerrigan said. Maybe the question should have been, "How in the world were you so prepared for a fastball?" Since my long-time strategy had worked, I told Kerrigan, "I've only seen one in my career, but I was ready for it."

Even after my conversation with Kerrigan, my search for fastballs from Wakefield continued. For any other hitter, that was a ridiculous strategy. But for me and for my mindset, that approach worked. Anticipating fastballs from a knuckleball pitcher made me comfortable that day and in subsequent days. And I had to be comfortable, even if that decision landed me in baseball's Dubious Hall of Fame.

CHAPTER 7

Ted Talks: Talking Hitting with Ted Williams

His voice was powerful and direct, kind of like the voice of God. In some ways, he was a god. A hitting god named Ted Williams calling my cell phone, as stunning and as welcome a call as I've ever received.

Flash back to spring training in late March 1999, where I was methodically getting ready for another day with the Yankees. Each spring, I would sweat and stew and take hundreds of reps as I searched for a swing that I could confidently carry into the regular season. But on this day in Tampa, I was ornery and sluggish because I was about 4 for my last 34. I wasn't balanced. I wasn't driving the ball. I was fighting the flu and I was miserable. And then my phone rang. And then the voice spoke.

"Paul? This is Ted Williams," the booming voice said. "I've been thinking about you. You're a hell of a ballplayer." Did I just hear him correctly? Was this really Ted Williams and did he really call me a hell of a player? Yes and yes. I placed my hand on the back of a chair, steadied myself, and sat down. My immediate reaction was to sit like a student in a classroom because I wanted to give this momentous call the respect it deserved.

I knew my sister, Molly, a reporter for *The New York Times*, was scheduled to interview Ted about food, fishing, and obviously, a little baseball, too. When Molly told me about her impending interview, I was excited for her and I was also in awe that my older sister was poised to speak with one of the greatest hitters of all time. I told Molly I was struggling and jokingly said she should tell Ted I needed some advice. Still, I never expected Molly's visit to Ted's home would result in him contacting me. This experience brought me back to being the boy whose proud father had told him his swing reminded him of Williams's swing. Well, I wasn't imitating Williams's swing anymore, but I was talking to the man himself.

To this day, even with my sister's connection and her gentle or forceful nudging, I'm still amazed that Ted was willing to call me. I was even more amazed when Ted said, "I bet you're not hitting the ball the other way." That comment gave me goose bumps because it showed that Ted knew the way that I had to hit to be a productive hitter. As I've stressed, to be successful, I needed to look for pitches on the middle and outside part of the plate and hit the ball to the opposite field. So, the legendary Ted Williams—a pull hitter who was also talented enough to adjust and hit the ball up the middle or the opposite way—knew my approach. The hitting genius knew my tricks.

"You know what?" I replied. "You're right. I've been getting out on my front side too quickly." A minute into the conversation, I was already trying to process how surreal it was that Ted Williams—*the Ted Williams*—was evaluating me as a hitter. Ted won six batting titles, two MVPs, made nineteen All-Star teams, was the last man to hit over .400 (in 1941), and finished his phenomenal career with a .344 average, 521 homers, and an all-time record .482 on-base percentage. He was the hero who also paused his career twice to serve our country in World War II and the Korean War. And he was talking to me about hitting! It was such an inspirational and nerve-racking call, because I was absorbing every word Ted uttered, but I also felt like there were a hundred questions I needed to ask before the voice of God hung up. I didn't want to interrupt and happily let him guide the conversation, and, perfectly and suddenly, Ted said something that made me smile.

"Don't let anybody change you!" Ted barked.

As much as any hitting advice I've ever received, those words resonated with me because they aligned with how I always felt. I've explained how I was stubborn and serious as a hitter and how I remained dedicated to my approach of swinging level and elevating into a slight uppercut and hitting line drives. But to hear Williams say that a hitter shouldn't let anyone change him, well, that was one of the highlights of the call. I just kept nodding as he said it. I could have listened to Ted repeat that sentence over and over.

Honestly, I should have expected Ted to emphasize that because it's what he had written in *The Science of Hitting*, his seminal book in which he dissected the most difficult thing to do in sports: hitting a baseball. I don't remember the first time I picked up the book, but I do remember being enamored with it. The book has a picture of Ted on the cover, his front foot slightly lifted, his eyes focused on the baseball, and body language that screams, "I'm about to crush this baseball!" Ted wrote that Lefty O'Doul, who batted .398 and had 254 hits in 1929 and had a .349 average during his eleven-year career, told him, "Son, whatever you do, don't let anybody change your style. Your style is your own." Ted obeyed. So did I.

As Ted continued to preach, he stressed the importance of having the best scouting report of all on myself. Basically, Ted said, I needed to know what I did well and work tirelessly to be superb at those things. I think that philosophy should apply to every athlete. It's a mistake to complicate things by trying to be something you're not or by trying to do something you're not capable of doing. "Know yourself as a hitter," Ted said. "Know who you are and what you can do and go do it. But you gotta know yourself."

Since I had always thought that batters need to be comfortable and confident in the way they hit, it was reassuring to hear Ted say the same thing. As I've mentioned, I always listened to the various voices that filled my world with hitting advice. But I was selective about which suggestions I actually adopted and added to my approach.

It's kind of humorous to concede this, but Ted's advice actually made me think about my boys. When I came home from Yankee Stadium after games, I would throw tennis balls to Aaron and Andy, just like my father did with me. But they were always trying to imitate Derek Jeter or Ken Griffey Jr. as we practiced. I understood that was just kids being kids, trying to be like their idols and the players they watched on television. I did the same thing with Pete Rose, Joe Morgan, and my heroes on the Big Red Machine. But after seeing dozens of Jeter and Griffey swings and few authentic Aaron and Andy swings, it would frustrate me because they weren't paying as much attention to their own hitting styles. "Just because you stand like Derek Jeter or swing like Ken Griffey Jr.," I would tell them, "doesn't mean you're going to hit like them."

Well, let's just say they didn't listen to me in the same way that I listened to my father or Ted. Like Ted, I really believed in being comfortable, from start to finish, when I was at the plate. Ted was so intelligent and so curious about hitting, even wondering if I had ever smelled the wood of the bat burning after a foul ball. I had. I've spoken to many people who don't believe hitters can smell the burnt wood when they connect on a pitch, but because of the friction of the leather against the wood, it is possible to smell it. It's the kind of smell that you'd get in the second or two after you try to light a match and the flame doesn't ignite.

In a rendezvous of three great hitting minds, Ted sat down with Wade Boggs and Don Mattingly in 1986 to talk hitting, and Peter Gammons of *Sports Illustrated* was there to describe the scene. At one point, Williams asked Boggs, "Have you ever smelled the wood from the bat burning?" Boggs was bewildered and said he had not. So, Williams said, "Five or six times, hitting against a guy with good stuff, I swung hard and—oomph—just fouled it back. Really hit it hard. And I smelled the wood of the bat burning. It must have been the seams that hit the bat just right, and the friction caused it to burn, but it happened five or six times." Boggs shook his head and just said, "Awesome," which was the only appropriate reaction.

Several months after Ted asked me that burning question, I saw him being treated like royalty while I was watching the highlights from the 1999 All-Star Game at Boston's Fenway Park. I had made the team in 1998, but I didn't make it in 1999. That was my loss. As soon as Williams was driven onto the center-field warning track in a green golf cart, the fans stood, screamed his name, and showed their appreciation for the great Red Sox hitter, one of the most prolific hitters of all time.

When Williams was brought to the mound to throw out the ceremonial first pitch, a beautiful and unplanned scene occurred. The All-Stars and the players who were on the field as part of the All-Century Team meandered toward Ted, like a bunch of seven-year-olds who were tiptoeing forward, shy and hesitant.

Mark McGwire, Cal Ripken Jr., Ken Griffey Jr., and Tony Gwynn, who credited Williams with helping him become better at handling inside pitches, all surrounded Ted. I saw Ted, that toughest of tough guys, wiping away tears as he spoke with the superstars of the day. As Ted vigorously chewed gum, he called to McGwire, who had walloped a then-record of 70 homers in the previous season. Williams put his right hand on McGwire's left shoulder and posed that familiar question.

"He asked me when I foul a ball off, do I smell burnt wood," McGwire revealed. "I said, 'All the time.'"

As astonished as I was while speaking with Ted, it was comforting to me that the conversation seamlessly became a chat between two hitters. Again, he was the expert. I did more listening than talking, but I did ask Ted what type of pitches he looked for in certain situations. It was enlightening to hear Ted say that he didn't like to swing at the first pitch of an at bat because he wanted to take some time to evaluate what type of pitches a pitcher had on a given day. Mostly though, Ted stressed the importance of getting a good pitch to hit. It sounds simple, but it's not.

Listening to Ted speak about swinging at good pitches reminded me of the part of his book that was most memorable to me: a rendering of the strike zone filled with rows of colored circles, detailing what Ted's expected batting average would be if he swung at a pitch in a certain area. There were eleven rows of circles with seven circles in each row, amounting to seventy-seven circles (or baseballs) that made up Ted's strike zone. Ted described a couple of circles right in the middle of the plate as his "happy zone," and he theorized he hit .400 while swinging at pitches in that juicy area. But there were also a few low and outside circles, and Ted thought he hit about .230 or .240 when he swung at pitches in that less desirable area. This was the type of math that spoke to me much more loudly than any of the classes I took in high school. Once I studied Ted's chart and the corresponding averages, it was a reminder of the value of swinging at strikes. Every batter has a sweet spot, a place where he knows he's going to do the most damage if he gets a pitch in that area. Again, for me, that place was typically a ball that was out over the plate.

Conversely, every batter has a weak area, too, a place that the opposition will inevitably uncover and try to exploit. The toughest pitch and location for me was a left-hander throwing a two-seam fastball that was inside and about waist-high. I had a difficult time picking that pitch up out of the pitcher's hand and didn't adjust to its right-to-left darting movement. Since I didn't bail out at the plate, I just had trouble getting to that pitch with my swing. If it was down and in, I had a much better chance of doing some damage. Sometimes, it was just necessary to be self-aware about the pitches I couldn't hit and lay off.

During one Yankees broadcast on the YES Network in 2021, Michael Kay, my friend and our play-by-play announcer, noted that Chipper Jones of the Atlanta Braves had named his son Shea after Shea Stadium, the Mets' old home, because he had performed so well in Flushing, New York. I chuckled at what Chipper did and decided to concoct my own different type of naming, one with a more negative connotation. If I had decided to name one of my sons after a pitch I couldn't hit, his birth certificate would have read: Lefty Two-Seamer O'Neill.

I dug my left foot into the back of the batter's box, I took a few practice swings, and I peered at the pitcher. I was ready to hit. But my focus was disturbed as I noticed that the Blue Jays' shortstop had shifted from his normal position and was now playing almost behind second base. Wait, what? As I've discussed, I wasn't a pull hitter so this move confused me. Why would the Jays play me to pull?

The Jays shifted against me during the 1994 season, a season that was never completed because of a work stoppage and a season in which I won a batting title by hitting .359 in 103 games for the Yankees. At the time, I was so angry that we never had the chance to finish a potentially special season that I wondered if the batting title was meaningless. To this day, I would have traded in that batting title for the chance to compete for a World Series title. The Yankees were 70-43 when the baseball season ended, an agonizing and deflating finish for so many.

Anyway, in the midst of my hitting splurge that season, the Jays used a new defensive strategy against me with their shortstop. Since the scouting report on me was that I preferred to hit the baseball to all fields, I figured they were shifting against me to try and get me to pull the ball. So, I braced myself for more inside pitches, but I didn't see a relentless diet of inside pitches. The Jays pitched me up and in and down and away and everywhere in between. They didn't just pound pitches on the inside corner, as I thought they would because of the shift. Now I was even more confused. Was I missing something?

That was a dreamy first half of the season for me as I took a .382 average into the All-Star Game break and made the American League team for the first time. I had previously played in one All-Star Game for the National League. Our starting outfield for the AL in that 1994 game was Griffey in center field, flanked by Joe Carter in left field, and Kirby Puckett in right field. I went 0 for 1 as a pinch hitter and the National League won 8-7 in ten innings.

One of the most critical developments of that All-Star experience occurred during a conversation with Cito Gaston, the Jays' manager, who managed the AL team because Toronto had won its second straight championship in 1993. Assuming I had nothing to lose in this more lighthearted setting, I approached Gaston and asked him a probing question.

"Why the heck do you shift against me?" I wondered.

Always cool and always coy, Gaston said, "You noticed it?"

"Of course, I noticed it," I told him.

"If you noticed it," Gaston replied, "then I've done my job."

That's when I understood what Gaston was doing. In essence, he was just trying to get inside my head and distract me while I was batting. And he's right. It worked. The shift did force me to think about things that I didn't want to think about while I was at the plate. If a pitcher or a team can distract a hitter in any way, well, that's a smart and effective strategy.

And guess what happened? After Gaston revealed Toronto's strategy to me, the Jays *still* played that modest shift against me. I continued to be surprised by it because I wasn't a pull hitter, but ultimately, I decided that I would use it to my advantage. While many current hitters obviously disagree with me based on their approach, I do believe that batters can beat shifts.

As the Yankees were valiantly fighting for a wild card spot on September 21, 1995, I batted against Toronto's Paul Menhart in the eighth inning. Bernie Williams was on first and we were down 4-1. I noticed Tomás Pérez, the shortstop, wasn't playing his usual position against me and was shaded much closer to second base. I refused to let Gaston or the Jays disrupt my focus with this subtle shift. I concentrated on hitting the ball the other way, which I did all the time anyway. I directed a grounder to where Pérez should have been playing and collected a single. If the shortstop hadn't shifted, it probably would have been a double play. I'm not sure if he noticed, but I gave Cito a smile when I got to first.

Rubén Sierra followed with a three-run homer, and we roared back to win 6-4. That comeback win was part of us winning 25 of our last 31 games that season. And we needed every one of those wins to qualify for the playoffs.

I've watched defensive shifts become more and more prominent in baseball in the last decade and rob hitters of an abundance of hits. Every hitter has tendencies, and opponents have spray charts that detail where he is most likely to hit the ball. If a left-handed slugger hits the ball to the right side the majority of the time, it's sensible and smart for a team to put an extra defender on that side. I understand that logic. But as I've said, hitters can conquer shifts if they really want to beat them. If a team is playing a lefty hitter to pull and has three infielders on the right side of the field, he can inside-out the ball to hit it the opposite way. There's an art to that type of hitting, but a hitter can spoil what a team is trying to do to him.

Some hitters, especially power hitters who pull the ball, aren't comfortable employing an inside-out swing because it's different from their regular swing. To use an inside-out swing, a batter must have quick and strong hands because he is waiting longer to swing as he is keeping the barrel behind his hands until it enters the hitting zone. But by using this inside-out swing, I could push the barrel of the bat through the zone and connect on pitches and send them to the opposite field. That's how a batter can beat a shift.

Teddy Ballgame knew a lot about trying to beat shifts because he faced one of the most drastic shifts in baseball history. After Williams went 4 for 5 with 3 homers and 8 RBIs in Game 1 of a doubleheader against Cleveland on July 14, 1946, Lou Boudreau, Cleveland's player-manager, defended Williams much differently in Game 2. Boudreau stationed seven of his eight fielders on the right side of the field, basically daring Williams to hit the ball to the left side. The only player on that side was a left fielder who was playing shallow in the outfield. Boudreau later admitted that the shift was a psychological ploy and that he hoped Williams, who considered himself the best hitter in baseball, would be too proud to make any adjustments.

While Joe Maddon and the Tampa Bay organization helped popularize the shift in the last decade and created a defensive revolution as every other major league team mimicked the strategy, shifting has been around for more than a century. Heck, Babe Ruth dealt with shifts, although they were in the outfield. Because teams have so much more information about opposing hitters these days, they sometimes even change the shift in the middle of an at bat.

In Ted's book, he noted that the shifts initially bothered him because he simply wasn't used to seeing that type of defense. But Ted was a hitting genius and a fierce competitor, so he discovered a solution to conquering the shift. "I survived," Williams said in *The Science of Hitting*, "by learning to hit to left field."

The transition wasn't easy. Ted was accused of being stubborn and hitting into the teeth of the shift too often, with certain hits turning into exasperating outs. When Ted finally devised a strategy for combating the shift, he would move his stance farther away from the plate, would stride more into the pitch, and would focus on hitting on top of the ball and pushing it. A push swing was an inside-out swing. By using that type of swing, Ted said it produced contact at ninety degrees or more from the pitch and sent the ball toward the left side of the pitcher and away from the dreaded shift.

When I read that Ted was all about beating the shift and not content with hitting into it like so many of today's hitters, it was so refreshing. If I were playing today, I would definitely devise a way to exploit a shift against me. At times, I must admit, I stare at the diamond during a game and see an infielder in shallow right field and I think, "Well, Ernie Banks never played out there. Neither did Phil Rizzuto." But, again, I also understand the logic of playing the fielders in the place where the hitter most consistently hits the ball.

When I debuted in the majors, I was always monitoring where the outfielders played, and as an outfielder, I had to shade to the left or to the right against certain hitters. Outfield shifts have been around forever, but those players are stationed a few hundred feet away from the batter. When the infielders started shifting so frequently because of the Rays' success, that became a much bigger story.

Even though I have heard an elite hitter like Mark Teixeira explain why he continued to hit the same way against the shift and why he didn't want to change his approach, the shift is beatable. It's a mindset of saying, "I'm going to stay inside the ball," if they are playing me to pull. But trust me, there's a way to do it. And once a hitter shows that he can beat the shift, the defense will have to shift back and play a normal defense.

It's no secret why most hitters refuse to be like Ted and make an adjustment against the shift: the home run is king and that's why many hitters focus on hitting the ball over the fence. I get it. Obviously, that's the way the game has trended and that's what's encouraged, because the homer is the most powerful way and the quickest way to produce runs. Players would prefer to hit the ball *over* the shift than try and imitate Derek Jeter or Rod Carew and slap the ball the other way. I wish it was different, but it isn't. I took a lot of pride in putting the ball in play and driving in runs. These days, the players are bigger and stronger and incredibly talented, and they have a lot of pride, too—but it's often reserved for when they blast three-run homers. Those blasts get standing ovations, as opposed to the polite applause for liners to where the shortstop should have been playing.

I still think a lot about that conversation with Ted. There are baseball players whose names are iconic because of what they accomplished. Ted Williams is one of those gigantic names. Every baseball player knows or should know the intimate details of Williams's Hall-of-Fame career. But to get a call from him? That's just unfathomable. If I had met Ted at a game and talked about hitting for a few minutes, that would have been cool and surreal, too. But there was something so phenomenal about having that one-on-one call. For those ten minutes or so, I had a personal hitting coach and his name was Ted Williams.

A few hours after the 1999 call, I was so invigorated in batting practice that I produced a bunch of squarely hit shots. And I kept telling myself, "If Ted Williams thinks I should be hitting the ball the other way, I'm going to make sure I'm hitting the ball the other way." Swing after swing, I worked diligently on smacking line drives to left-center field that day. After every well-placed liner, I heard Ted's authoritative voice telling me that I was doing exactly what I needed to do as a hitter.

Ted left me with these final pieces of advice: "Wait for your pitch," Williams added. "And remember, the lousier you're hitting, the more you're thinking about hitting. You shouldn't have a worry in the world. I'm telling you right now. You're a hell of a player."

Yes, I heard it right. Ted Williams called me a hell of a player. I think I could have retired that day and been a happy man. Oh, and after my conversation with Ted, I ripped two line drives to the opposite field that night. I felt like a hell of a ballplayer.

CHAPTER 8

Truths from Torre

The Yankees' clubhouse was unusually serene on this spring-training day. Typically, the players' home away from home is bustling as we get prepared for workouts or games and shout across the room to each other. There is music playing and the TV is locked-in on a game or a sports highlight show. And normally, players are laughing, smiling, and bonding.

But on this February day in 1996, we were subdued as we sat in folding chairs inside our spring home in Tampa, Florida. We were bracing for some important words, so, like a bunch of students who realized we should be polite for the teacher, we sat quietly and waited. We waited for Joe Torre to address us as a group for the first time.

I had never met Joe before he became manager of the Yankees, and I was curious about what he might say. Before Torre started the meeting, here's what I knew about him: He had been a superb hitter and a player I enjoyed watching. He had managed the New York Mets, the Atlanta Braves, and the St. Louis

Cardinals (against me and the Cincinnati Reds). He wasn't the Yankees' first choice to replace Buck Showalter. I also read that George Steinbrenner, the owner who hired Torre, immediately grew antsy about the decision and secretly visited with Showalter with the thought of rehiring him. Torre's job title might have been switched to an unhappy adviser. But none of those details mattered to Torre. He was excited about getting a wonderful opportunity, however it evolved.

From the opening words of Joe's speech, I was entranced because he spoke the language of a player. He spoke my language. He spoke Tino Martinez's language. He spoke Bernie Williams's language. He capably and carefully described what it was like to be a player, from the exhilarating games to the exasperating games, and instantly proved that he understood us. "I want you to know I've been in your shoes and I know what it's like to have good days and bad days," I remember Torre saying. "And, when that happens to you, I'll understand it because I've been there and I've lived it, too."

Treating the clubhouse like a classroom, Joe told us he hit .363 and won a batting title in 1971 and he hit .247 and lost a lot of sleep in 1975. And he tried just as hard in those two seasons. It was a strong message about what we can and can't control. As someone who was perpetually demanding of himself and who couldn't fully understand the reasons for my struggles, Joe's words resonated with me. This is a hard game. And sometimes, you're not going to outwork, outmuscle, or outlast some negative results. Sometimes, an opponent will defeat you, no matter how much you prepared.

In discussing his career as a player and a manager and

how he'd worked in Milwaukee, Atlanta, St. Louis, and New York, I was half-expecting Torre to quote lyrics from a Johnny Cash song and say, "I've been everywhere, man." Again, it was refreshing to hear Joe talk about the circuitous road that had led a kid from Brooklyn to become the manager of the renowned team in the Bronx. At the age of fifty-five, and as someone who had been dismissed from three different managerial jobs, Joe wasn't sure he would ever manage again.

I wasn't always fond of team meetings. There were times I would get fidgety because I felt like I should be taking some swings in the batting cage or lifting some weights or doing something that would be more beneficial. But Joe's meeting? This meeting was different and had some crucial messages. Joe wanted to let us know who he was and where he had been, that he understood us, that we would have his unwavering support, and that he, and no one else, would be the person making the on-field decisions.

"You don't know what's going to happen when you have that type of meeting," Torre said. "You hope you accomplish what you wanted to accomplish. You want to be able to connect with people. Like I said, connecting with the players was the most important thing.

"There were certain things they had to know, especially since I was working for George Steinbrenner and the Yankees," Torre explained. "Sure, I had a boss. But they had to know I was making the baseball decisions. Nobody was writing the lineup for me. I thought it was important they knew that and that no one was dictating decisions to me and my coaches."

There was one other valuable and overriding message that

Joe delivered: he was managing the Yankees to win it all. After thirty-two years as a player and a manager, Torre had never been to a World Series. He mentioned how all of his coaches had enjoyed that experience as players, and he wanted an invite to that October bash. And then Joe said something that was brash, exciting, and daring: "I don't want to win just one," Joe told us. "I want to win three in a row. I want to establish something special here." Was Torre the greatest motivator ever or just delusional? Shockingly, we did exactly what Joe had prophesied by winning it all in 1996, his first year, and following that up by winning three straight titles in 1998, 1999, and 2000.

Any time Joe spoke, he had my undivided attention because his words were impactful. If someone gathered the transcripts from Joe's clubhouse speeches and published a book, it would have been a best-seller for inspiration.

As Torre began evaluating his players, someone in the organization told him I was a "selfish" player. It was bothersome to hear that someone viewed me that way. I was passionate and stubborn, and I had personal goals like hitting .300 and driving in 100 runs, but my focus was on winning. And I've always been grateful that Joe recognized that about me.

"I never bought into this idea that he was selfish," Torre said. "I found out he's selfish in the way that he wants to get a hit every time up. And that was fine with me. I would take twenty-five hitters like that." Joe was a player's manager and clearly, he understood me. "Paul was such a great hitter and he wore his heart on his sleeve," Torre said. "He was so passionate about it. One thing about Paul O'Neill is that he never blamed anybody. He would always act out, but whatever he did, he never blamed anyone. It was all geared toward him. He never blamed anyone but himself."

Several hours after Joe's initial speech, I know exactly where I was and what I was doing. I was standing in my Tampa apartment and mimicking my stance, because I did the same thing in the first two weeks of every spring training, a ritual that started in 1993. I would practice my leg kick every night because that was vital preparation for the upcoming season.

That meant I would retreat to a quiet room, lift my front leg up, and stop, holding my leg in the position where I was still balanced and was ready to hit. And, each night, I would just hold my leg in that position over and over. I wanted to get acclimated to that approach, so I would do this ten, twenty, or thirty times, or however long it took for me to feel comfortable.

In Cincinnati, I was an old-school hitter who just stood tall and then stepped toward the pitcher with my front foot. Because I'm six feet four, one of my big flaws was I drifted forward and my body kind of tipped. When that happened, my head and my hands would be out of position and I would force everything to happen a little quicker with my swing. When a batter drifts like that, it doesn't give him time to recognize the pitch and adjust to it, and he can't get the bat in the proper position to hit the baseball squarely. We only have about four-tenths of a second to hit the ball, and drifting slices into that precious time.

If I could put my leg in that lifted position and be poised every time the ball left the pitcher's hand, I was giving myself the best chance to hit. If I was late with my leg kick, then I would be tilting forward again. If I was early, it was hard to stay balanced. When I struggled with my timing, I would become maniacal about correcting it during batting practice. As soon as the pitcher removed his hand from his glove and dropped his arm, my leg needed to be in the air. The timing was practically a ballet move. And after working on that in BP, I would, hopefully, bring the refined version of my leg kick into the game.

Even before I was traded to the Yankees, I had already decided I was going to implement a leg kick for the 1993 season. That change was inspired by watching Juan González of the Texas Rangers. González was a fearless hitter who always seemed to be in a balanced position because of his leg kick. I was envious of that and wondered if I would be able to employ a leg kick and keep my balance. I had seen other hitters do it, but could I? Fortunately, I discovered that I could keep my balance, even as I was standing on one leg during my swing. I would tap my front foot before I lifted it, which was a way to get my foot in motion as I waited on the pitcher.

Fortunately, I had a smart and supportive batting coach in Rick Down to help me with this adjustment. Rick was stocky, with thick forearms and a prodigious work ethic, which I appreciated. He had endured more than a dozen knee surgeries and walked with a limp, but he moved around the batting cage with enthusiasm. Nudging me, advising me, and guiding me.

As I reflect on those cage sessions and developing that leg kick, I must say that Rick loved the work as much as I did. And that's quite a compliment, because I was obsessed with making my leg kick work. During hundreds of swings where my timing had to be precise, he'd be beside me with his words of wisdom. Like I said, my mantras were, "Stay on top of the ball," and, "Hit the ball hard," to help me stay focused at the plate. Rick knew that and he'd yell those reminders to me.

Of course, the ultimate test was using the leg kick in a game. I could stare at a mirror and balance myself on one leg for a hundred hours, but that wasn't relevant unless I could succeed with it when I swung. Once a hitter tries something different, whether it's a modified stance or a swing adjustment, it's so crucial to have early success. Until the change produces results, there will be some doubts.

But those doubts didn't last long, because the leg kick ended up working for me. After a few unsteady at bats in which I wasn't getting my leg into position in a timely manner, I faced Mike Bielecki in my third game as a Yankee. On a 1-1 pitch, I lifted my leg at the precise time, stayed balanced, and hit the ball over the right-field fence for my first homer in pinstripes.

The leg kick is a timing mechanism, so it's not always going to be exact and it requires discipline to make it work. The homer was nice, but the execution of the leg kick was just as important. I knew I'd found a new way to hit.

Everything I did with the leg kick was predicated on when the pitcher released the ball. Pitchers who used a slide step or who quick-pitched me could disrupt my timing. In one at bat against Tom Candiotti, a knuckleball pitcher, I started my leg kick and realized he had a slow delivery—he hadn't even released the ball yet. I quickly lowered my leg to the dirt and lifted it back up again to be ready for Candiotti's pitch. But that was a rare experience. Most of the time, I was comfortable with my leg kick. Once I became comfortable with it, I wondered how I had ever hit without it. "The way that Paul hit, I loved seeing it," Torre said. "He was balanced up there. He could hit a line drive to left. He could hit a shot to center field. He could hook one down the right-field line.

"As a catcher, I found it so tough to try and pitch to Roberto Clemente or Hank Aaron because they could hit the ball to all parts of the field," Torre continued. "With hitters like that, there's only a little spot, if that, where you might be able to get them out. I felt the same way about Paul when I watched him hit. There weren't a lot of areas where they could attack him. His ability to take a level swing and hit the ball to left field, that really stood out. And to be able to wait as long as he waited to swing, that was key for him. He could let the ball get really deep, which I really admired and which made him tough to pitch to."

Sitting on a long aluminum bench that was attached to the back of the batting cage, Joe watched over our pregame swings. If Joe spoke during BP, it was usually encouraging and lighthearted. But Joe knew I didn't do lighthearted very well. Even in BP, I had a plan of attack. If I faced 15 pitches in a round of BP, I would try to get loose for the first seven or eight and start to feel good about my swing. Then, I would put myself into game situations for a few pitches and imagine there was a runner on third base with one out and I needed to knock him in. Then I would try to hit a line drive single or hit a ball in the air for a sacrifice fly. I couldn't create those game situations on every pitch because it's impossible to trick your mind that often, but I did it enough to get me ready for the game.

It was always comforting to see Joe and Don Zimmer, his trusted bench coach, behind the cage. But I wasn't a jokester when it came to hitting. I took BP very seriously. One day, Joe called me into his office and said, "You do know that BP is to get loose, right? And you do know it's no indication of what you're going to do in the game?" I understood what Torre meant, but to me, my BP swings could be indicative of what I might do. Sometimes, my most pivotal at bat could happen in the first inning and I wanted to be ready for that at bat. If I didn't feel right after several rounds of outdoor BP, I would sneak down to the indoor cage and keep swinging until I was satisfied.

"The game takes enough out of you," Torre said. "I didn't like to see guys get a little drained before it was for real. Paul took batting practice the way he was going to approach the game. Pete Rose did the same thing. And I respected that and I admired that. What I was telling Paul is that there's only so much gas in the tank. I didn't want him to lose a gallon before he went out there for nine innings."

My level of seriousness with BP extended to the pitchers I faced. If the BP pitcher was having an inconsistent day, that frustrated me. I loved Willie Randolph, a former Yankee All-Star and one of our dedicated coaches, but his fastballs would cut and sink, and it felt like I was being challenged by a nasty reliever. I would chirp at Willie, "You're exhausting me up here!"

For throwing hittable fastballs in perfect locations, my

favorite BP pitcher was Mike Borzello, a lanky, wise-cracking right-hander. Everyone called him "Borzy," and he'd throw straight fastball after straight fastball, which is what I wanted. Borzy, who was Torre's godson, was machine-like in beautifully locating the baseball every time. Fifteen of Borzy's pitches equaled 15 strikes and 15 more chances for me to get myself ready for the game.

Since I faced Borzy every day, he knew my hitting tendencies and my moods as well as any of my teammates. There was a camaraderie between us, as Borzy saw all the highs and lows of my hitting journey on a daily basis. To thank Borzello for those hundreds of perfect fastballs, I would give him a nice bonus at the end of the season.

While having a strong season in 1997, I decided to have some fun with Borzy. If I hit .320 or better, I told Borzy his bonus would be a certain amount. But, if I hit under .320, his bonus would be lower. Baseball seasons are a very long grind, so this was a fun way to motivate me and my BP pitcher. And Borzy took this challenge seriously.

In our second-to-last game of the season, I was batting exactly .320, so Borzy was on the cusp of getting the larger bonus. With only a handful of at bats left for me, one at bat could have meant the difference between Borzy getting some money and a bigger chunk of money. I notched two early hits in that game and boosted my average to .322. The better payday was getting closer and closer.

With two outs and a runner on second in the seventh inning, the Tigers brought in Mike Myers, a side-arming left-hander, to oppose lefty-hitting Wade Boggs. I was on deck. If

Boggs reached base, I would have had to face Myers, whose funky, low-angle delivery made it difficult for a lefty to pick up the baseball. I ended up 1 for 7 off Myers in my career.

Anyway, realizing I might have to face a situational lefty who was as tough on lefties as anyone in the majors, Borzy, who was also a bullpen catcher, panicked and used the bullpen phone to call Torre in the dugout. "I don't think O'Neill needs this at bat right now," Borzello told Torre. With the playoffs looming, Joe presumed Borzy's rationale was to protect me from disrupting my mechanics against a difficult lefty.

While Borzy presented it that way, he was also looking out for my average and for his bonus. I didn't face Myers, as Boggs lined out, but Torre was planning to replace me against Myers—he used Chad Curtis, a right-handed batter, to pinch-hit for me against right-hander Eddie Gaillard in the eighth. My average stayed at .322, and I added two more hits in the final game to finish at .324.

I smiled. Borzy smiled. And I gave Borzy the larger bonus.

Like many hitters, I was a creature of habit. I liked to do things in a certain way and at a certain time, which included watching a version of my greatest hits before every game. Videotaped scouting and analysis was only becoming popular toward the end of my career, but I watched a ton of video of my swing in my last several years.

I would chronicle the at bats in which I felt I had perfect swings, and then I'd ask Charlie Wonsowicz, our video coordinator and a street-smart New Yorker, to compile those at bats on one tape. They weren't all homers. Not even close. There would be five line drives up the middle, five more bullets to left-center, and five more rockets to right-center. These at bats came against pitches I felt I had handled and where I felt great about the swing. It was roughly 15 at bats, but I would study them back-to-back-to-back, and those at bats would resonate with me because I would see, over and over, what I had done technically to produce that result.

About fifteen or twenty minutes before a game started, I would sit in front of the TV screen and stare at my swings because those at bats were examples of exactly what I wanted to do. I wasn't just collecting hits on pitches that were down the middle, either. Sometimes, it would be an outside pitch that I laced to left. Sometimes, it would be an inside pitch and I stayed on it and drove it to right. By repeatedly watching my swings, I put myself in a much stronger mindset.

And hitting is definitely a mind game. That's why I always included at least one recent at bat because that experience would be fresh in my memory and would add to my confidence. Once I saw that at bat from a day or two earlier, it would tell me that I'd swung the bat well at least once recently, even if I was struggling.

Dozens of times, I would walk into the video room and holler, "I've got another one to add to the tape, Chuck." And Charlie, who was also our lefty BP pitcher, would edit the tape and add another one of my smash hits. Every time I watched myself make contact on that three-minute tape, I reinforced what I had accomplished. That's how I forced myself to envision positive results. If I didn't sit down and watch that tape before a game, I'd freak out. I needed to watch it to feel ready for the game. "It was interesting, because we didn't have the type of technology that hitters have today," Wonsowicz said. "But Paul always wanted to watch that tape."

How obsessed was I with my swing? As I stood in right field, I would frequently practice my swing during lulls in the action. This was all about visualization. The more you visualize what you want to do, the better chance you have of doing it. If I swung enough, even as I was positioned in the outfield, I almost trained my brain to think of only one thing. And when you're hitting, the fewer thoughts you have, the better off you are. If you can visualize enough about what you want to do with your mechanics and put yourself in the same spot on every single pitch, then you have given yourself the best chance to hit something hard.

I know I was in the extreme minority as a player who took swings while he was on defense. Naturally, that led to teasing from my teammates. Brian Boehringer, a reliever, once said, "I used to look out in right field and I'd see you practicing hitting." Then he paused and added, "But I've never looked in the on-deck circle and seen you practicing fielding."

I had no comeback. He was right. Nonetheless, I kept doing it.

Sheepishly, I must admit my fanaticism with swinging in the outfield became problematic during Game 5 of the 1996 World Series. With pinch hitter Luis Polonia batting and runners on the corners in the ninth inning, we had a 1-0 lead over the Braves. For some unknown reason, I decided to practice my swing during the tensest moment of the season. Like I said, I always thought it was smart to visualize what I wanted to do at the plate. But two outs in the ninth inning of a World Series game? Old habits die hard, I guess.

The issue with me swinging an imaginary bat in that situation was that José Cardenal, one of our coaches, was trying to get my attention. I wasn't looking toward the first-base dugout, so I didn't see him motioning to me. Finally, in between my practice swings, I spotted Cardenal waving a white towel and I thought, "Is he trying to tell me something?" He was. Cardenal wanted me to shift about eight feet to my right.

By the time I moved, Polonia had already fouled off three of John Wetteland's fastballs. Polonia fouled off three more pitches, the anxiety heightening with each pitch. On the seventh pitch of the at bat, Polonia hit a shot toward right-center field. Initially, I thought I had the ball fairly easily, but then it soared on me and I said, "Oh, my God."

Scaring me even more was the reality that I was playing on a severely strained left hamstring and, at best, I was running at about 70 percent of my capacity. Every time I made a quick or sudden movement, I felt a stabbing pain in my hammy.

Sprinting as fast as my legs would allow, I hustled on a forty-five-degree angle toward where I thought the ball would be, stretched, and barely snared it in my outstretched glove. I crossed the warning track, smacked my palm against the wall, and screamed in delight. As a gimpy thirty-three-year-old who was 6 for 35 in the playoffs, making that catch was the most important play I made in October.

"If Paul doesn't move," Cardenal said, "I don't think he catches that ball." Cardenal was right. I wouldn't have caught Polonia's shot if I stayed in the same spot, especially with an ailing hamstring.

"He caught the ball on one leg," Torre said. "If he doesn't

catch it, we lose that game and we might have even lost the series."

Several years later, Derek Jeter mentioned how my catch changed the whole complexion of the series and how it could have even changed the complexion of the future for those Yankee teams.

Indeed. Before we could win four championships in five years, we had to win the first one. We accomplished that two nights later when we overcame the masterful Greg Maddux and won 3-2. After we lost the first two games at the Stadium by a combined score of 16-1 and felt embarrassed and disrespected, Torre, the master of motivation, met with Steinbrenner in the manager's officer at Yankee Stadium. Very calmly and very confidently, Joe told a concerned Steinbrenner that Atlanta was his old baseball home, and he was sure we would win three straight games there and then win Game 6 in New York to clinch the series. And we did.

In a scoreless Game 6, I led off the third inning against Maddux, a brilliant control artist. Maddux's best pitch was a two-seam fastball that would look as if it was about to nick a left-handed hitter in the hip before sharply darting from the left to the right for a strike. I hated getting into two-strike counts against Maddux because he was so cunning and had so many weapons.

Sure enough, Maddux threw me a fastball, a change-up, and another fastball, which I was late on and fouled off, to jump ahead 1-2. Maddux tried to bury me with another change and it was a terrific pitch, but I barely checked my swing and stayed alive in the at bat. When Maddux tossed a sinker, it stayed inside and up and I lashed it into the right-field corner for a double. That pitch wasn't nearly as good as Maddux's previous pitch, and by staying inside the ball and not opening up too soon, I was able to connect with it.

After Mariano Duncan's groundout pushed me to third, Joe Girardi, who had caught Maddux with the Chicago Cubs, was the next batter. With the infield in, Joe knew Maddux would be aggressive and try to get ahead in the count. He jumped on Maddux's first pitch, a two-seamer that was up, and hammered it to center. Marquis Grissom was playing extremely shallow and didn't come close to catching a ball that bounced off the warning track. As I excitedly trotted home on Girardi's triple, it was the first time I had ever felt the ground shake at the Stadium. I'm not exaggerating. When my foot touched the plate, I thought there was a tremor in the Bronx.

Jeter and Bernie added run-scoring singles in that inning as we built a 3-0 lead and held on tight for the win. I can still see Mark Lemke's foul pop-up along the third-base line landing in Charlie Hayes's glove for the final out, which unleashed a raucous celebration in front of 56,375 fans. Wetteland leaped into Girardi's arms and more players smothered them, and within a few seconds, there were about fifteen bodies stacked on the infield grass. Since I had to dash in from right, I was late to the celebration, so I dove onto the pinstriped pile, bounced off Bernie's back, and landed on the ground. I was relieved we didn't have a game the next day, because my back was pretty sore following my Bronx leap.

In the moments after we won, I thought of Torre, our stoic and soothing leader. It took him thirty-two years, but he finally had a World Series ring. As we hugged, I could see the joy and relief in Joe's face following such an emotional year. One day before we clinched the title, Joe's brother Frank had received a successful heart transplant. Four months earlier, his other brother Rocco died of a heart attack.

But throughout all his family's anguish, Joe never lost confidence in us or himself. I remember how he constantly said, "*When* we win the World Series," and not, "*If* we win it." The phrasing might not seem like much of a difference, but the players in our clubhouse noticed it and were strengthened by it.

There were so many wonderful aspects of that 1996 season, a season where I hit .302 with a .411 on-base percentage, a .474 slugging percentage, and 19 homers and 91 runs batted in. Dwight Gooden, who had been a Mets icon, pitched a no-hitter against a powerful Seattle lineup in his seventh start with us. David Cone returned from life-threatening aneurysm surgery to win a series-turning Game 3 against the Braves. Darryl Strawberry, another former Met, overcame substance abuse issues to resurrect his career and make Steinbrenner look smart for believing in him. And Torre and Jeter, two future Hall of Famers, were as perfect as a first-year manager and a first-year shortstop could be.

But one of my most vivid memories about that season happened a few days after we won it all. At the championship parade along Broadway, the full power of the Yankees' fan base hit me with the force of a hundred consecutive walk-off celebrations.

During the season, I lived in Rye Brook, New York, in

Westchester County. For my commute, I would drive about a half hour to Yankee Stadium, play in front of about 40,000 people, and drive back home. I witnessed the passion of Yankee fans on a daily basis and was impressed with their intensity and their knowledge. I knew the Yankees were the most renowned franchise in baseball, and I knew there were a lot more fans than the people I saw each night, but I guess I just never really calculated how many. Until that parade.

Standing on a blue-and-white parade float, I saw people in Yankee T-shirts and Yankee jackets and Yankee caps, lined up for what seemed like miles, and it gave me the chills. I actually used a camcorder to preserve the memories, and the whole experience was unreal. With confetti, toilet paper, and blank credit-card receipts falling from the sky and this sea of Yankee humanity screaming at us, the decibel level was as deafening as a plane taking off. And taking off again. And taking off again.

Those sights and sounds awed me into realizing how many millions and millions of people lived and died with what the Yankees did. This Columbus kid feels sheepish admitting that it took a parade along the Canyon of Heroes for me to fully grasp the depth of Yankee fandom, but that parade truly taught me about the length, the breadth, and the width of the New York faithful. Heck, the Rockettes and the Village People were even part of the celebration. Now that's a party!

I didn't have to swing a bat or throw a ball that day, but seeing fans weeping with joy or hanging out of office windows or sitting on each other's shoulders shook me for a long moment. I asked myself, "Were these millions of people really watching us that closely?" And obviously, they were. I was part of a championship parade with the Reds in 1990, but it was an afternoon tea compared to this rowdy block party, or, more aptly, blocks party. I didn't want it to end.

It's hard to express too much frustration about our dynastic run, but 1997 was such an exasperating finish for us. While I thought we were as talented in 1997 as we were in 1996, we lost to Cleveland in five games in the American League Division Series. I wish my two-out, line-drive double off José Mesa in the ninth inning had climbed a bit higher and tied the game. Instead, it was several feet short.

In the clubhouse afterward, Torre, the man with all the inspirational speeches, didn't say a word. It was another one of Joe's notable meetings, but this was a silent meeting. He sat on a chair in the middle of the room and shared the pain of the loss with us. The silence lasted for about fifteen minutes. Eventually, Joe hugged all of us and said thank-you. He didn't need to speak. We were the 1996 champions who fell short in 1997.

Sometimes, like many professional athletes, I wallow in the painful losses more than I revel in the glorious wins. I felt sickened when we lost in 1995 and I felt just as queasy when we lost in 1997. But I do think what happened in 1997 emboldened us to come back and perform at an extremely high level. Bernie Williams, who made the final out of that playoff series against Cleveland, spent the off-season thinking about that out and said that he would never let that happen again. Bernie was motivated to excel. We all were. The incredible 1998 started because we were so disappointed with 1997.

I'm not breaking news when I say that the 1998 Yankees were the best team I ever played on, and maybe the best team of all time. We were professional, selfless, determined, and talented. We were a team's team. I'm going to steal something that David Cone has said about that club: When you analyze the team from players one through twenty-five, it's possible to argue that it's the best-constructed roster of all time. Other teams had more future Hall of Famers, other teams probably had more talent in the top echelon of players, but our team was filled with useful and versatile players who just fit together so perfectly and seamlessly. On certain days, our bench included Tim Raines, a future Hall of Famer, and Strawberry, who pounded over 300 homers.

We started the season 1-4, and there were some rumors about Torre being in trouble and possibly even being fired, which was laughable. Before our sixth game, yes, our sixth game, Joe had a memorable team meeting in Seattle in which we talked about challenging ourselves and about the Mariners disrespecting us. The soft-tossing Jamie Moyer had inadvertently hit me with a pitch in the series, and, because of the Lou Piniella factor, we used that as a rallying cry, too.

We won that night and we kept winning and winning. We rushed to a 61-20 record at the halfway point of the season, becoming only the third team ever to do that. The more we won, the more invincible we became. There were numerous times when we scored early in games and I think the opponents actually relented and determined it wasn't their day. We were a classy bunch, but an intimidating bunch.

On a sunny Sunday in May, the 17th to be exact, I was

positioned in right field and watching in amazement as David Wells mesmerized the Minnesota Twins. The durable Wells had an excellent assortment of pitches, he worked quickly, and, most of all, he threw strike after strike and pounded the zone. When I faced Wells, he would throw me inside fastballs and then get me to chase curves or cutters off the plate. I could never figure him out. Neither could the Twins as Wells retired the first 26 batters of the game.

"One more out, Boomer," I thought to myself, as Wells faced Pat Meares. And suddenly, Meares swung and the ball was flying toward me. I only had to slide a few steps to my left to catch this routine fly-out. I corralled it with my right hand and pumped my fist with my left. I hung on to the prized final out of perfection and gave the baseball to Wells in the clubhouse.

I wasn't perfect in 1998, but I did hit over .300 for the sixth straight season. Still, I was seeing the ball so well that Torre called me into the visiting manager's office at Fenway Park one afternoon to talk hitting. As talented a hitter as Joe was, and as much as he knew about hitting, he didn't regularly talk hitting with his players because he respected and trusted his coaches. But Joe and I gathered in the cramped office and that's when he said, "You're doing a great job of covering the baseball."

That comment resonated with me. In fact, Joe's words brought me back to my teenage days with Ted Kluszewski, the Reds' minor-league hitting instructor, who would say, "You left me," when I failed to cover an outside pitch and hit it to left field. Ted was always telling me to stay with the pitch, to cover it, and to hit it hard. When a hitter doesn't do that, he comes around the ball and tries to pull it and he won't hit it with as much authority.

From his perch in the dugout, Joe had recognized exactly what I was doing in staying with pitches and driving them. If Torre had talked hitting with me every day, his comments wouldn't have been as meaningful. But since it happened infrequently, it felt like the teacher told me I was getting an A in class.

Our 1998 season was taken from the pages of a baseball fairy tale, as we won 114 games in the regular season and were overwhelming favorites to win another title. As formidable as we had been for six months, we all knew we had to win the title to be remembered as a legendary team. Baseball history is filled with teams who had excellent regular seasons and then sputtered in the postseason, from the 1954 Cleveland Indians (111-43) to the 1931 Philadelphia A's (107-45) to the 1906 Chicago Cubs (116-36). Those teams didn't win it all. We needed to finish the deal.

Our greatest postseason obstacle occurred after we fell behind Cleveland two games to one in the American League Championship Series. Orlando Hernández saved our season by pitching seven scoreless innings in a 4-0 win in Game 4. I clubbed a homer off Gooden, my old teammate, in the first inning for our first run and walked and scored another run in the fourth. But the pitcher known as El Duque was spectacular in the most pressure-filled start of the season. We won the next two games to advance to the World Series, as we all had expected.

We swept the San Diego Padres in four games, cementing our status as an all-time legendary team. I felt a mixture of joy and relief as Jeter and I poured champagne on Steinbrenner's head in a steamy clubhouse. Even as we celebrated, we dedicated the win to Strawberry, our teammate who missed the playoffs while fighting colon cancer. As the champagne flowed, reporters asked if we were the greatest team of all time. I didn't see the 1927 Yankees, the 1939 Yankees, or the 1961 Yankees, and the little boy in me has an affinity for the Big Red Machine championship teams in 1975 and 1976, but I would say our 1998 team could compete with any of those teams.

Not surprisingly, I was asked countless questions about my teammates after that 1998 season. Whether I was in a restaurant, on an airplane, or at one of my kids' school functions or games, fans wanted to know anything and everything about some of my talented teammates. I always answered their questions, but I saved some of my favorite anecdotes and stories until now.

Let's start at the end, which means I'm starting with Mariano Rivera, the closer. While he was the greatest closer ever and is one of the main reasons the Yankees excelled in the postseason, I marveled at how humble and unflappable Mariano was. Honestly, his humility was staggering. Mo was a deeply religious man who never boasted, who always talked about "we" over "I," and who was focused on winning. As humble and as kind as Mo was, I must emphasize that he was a piranha on the mound. In his surgical way, he wanted to decimate batters with that amazing cutter.

In our years as teammates, I had only one recurring complaint about Mariano: "Hey, Mo," I would say playfully, "do you really have to shag fly balls with us during batting practice?" As part of his pregame conditioning, Mariano would glide around the outfield like a Gold Glover and snare fly balls. Rivera was a pitcher, but he was also one of the best athletes on the team, so he made us real outfielders look like stand-ins. "Go back to the bullpen!" I would scream. "That's supposed to be the place where you hang out."

Countless times in BP, I would take a few steps toward right-center to field a liner. And another player would soar past me and smoothly make the catch. I would wonder, "Was that Bernie?" Nope, it wasn't our Gold Glove center fielder making the play. It was our All-World closer.

We also had an All-World shortstop in Jeter, the player who received the most unique applause of any of my teammates. When Jeter strolled to the plate, the young fans wouldn't cheer as much as they would squeal. It was the epitome of kids being excited, and there's nothing louder or cooler than that. Since Jeter used to tease me about being eleven years older than him, I would admit defeat and say, "Jete, you've got the little kids on your side. But I've got the grandmas and grandpas rooting for me."

Our age difference caused Jeter and me to have some humorous exchanges about music, too. During spring training in 1998, he was blasting Will Smith's "Gettin' Jiggy Wit It" and bouncing around our clubhouse. That song spent three weeks at number one on the Billboard Hot 100 chart starting in March, but I had one pertinent question for Jeter: "Getting jiggy with it?" I asked him. "What does that even mean?"

It was thrilling to attend my first major league game as a seven-year-old. I wore my Reds helmet and even showed off my batting stance. Naturally, I cheered for my Reds against the Pirates, but my father also made sure the legendary Roberto Clemente was in the background of this picture. I'm grateful he did. (Courtesy of Paul O'Neill)

As a boy, I took thousands of swings in my backyard and dreamed of becoming a major leaguer. And that dream came true when I debuted with the Reds, the team I always adored, on September 3, 1985. I feel thankful and blessed that I lived out my dream. (Courtesy of the Cincinnati Reds)

Eight days after my debut, I watched Pete Rose collect his 4,192nd career hit and break Ty Cobb's all-time record. I joined my teammates on the field to congratulate the Hit King. If you look real closely, you might see the back of my head near Pete's right shoulder in this picture. (Focus on Sport via Getty Images)

I was in the middle of this Reds' celebration after we won the 1990 NLCS over the Pirates. I hit .471 with a homer in my first postseason series. Soon after, we swept Oakland in four games and won the World Series. It was a remarkable feeling to win a title with my home-town team. (Courtesy of Chuck Solomon/*Sports Illustrated* via Getty Images.)

I implemented a leg kick before the 1993 season, and that timing mechanism allowed me to become a more comfortable and more confident hitter. Across my nine seasons with the Yankees, my leg kick helped me to a .303 average, 185 homers, and an .869 OPS. (Courtesy of Otto Gruele/ Allsport via Getty Images)

I spent a lot of time around batting cages with Don Mattingly when we were Yankee teammates. While Cap was wearing his Marlins uniform and I was wearing jeans and a shirt in this picture, I guarantee we were still talking about hitting. Tim Wallach, who was one of Mattingly's coaches, was also with us. (Courtesy of Mark Brown/Getty Images)

Joe Torre was the always-intelligent and always-soothing manager for all four of my World Series titles with the Yankees. Joe understood the highs and lows of being a player and connected with all of us. And when Joe talked, I listened. Especially when the former batting champ gave me hitting advice. (Courtesy of Doug Kanter/AFP via Getty Images)

After we defeated the Braves and won the 1996 World Series, I ran in from right field to join the celebration. Since I was a little late to the party, I decided to crash it by diving on top of the pile. I love this picture, but I didn't love the back soreness I felt the next day. (Courtesy of Linda Cataffo/New York *Daily News* via Getty Images)

I shared dugouts with a lot of phenomenal players, and Derek Jeter and Mariano Rivera were at the top of that list. Both were elected to the Hall of Fame on their first ballots. They were talented, confident, and dedicated and had a tremendous impact on their teammates and our teams. (Courtesy of Keith Torre/New York *Daily News* via Getty Images)

Once we secured the final out of the 1999 World Series victory over the Braves, I was mentally and physically drained. I briefly congratulated my teammates, but I began to weep and dashed to the dugout. My father had passed away hours earlier, and I wanted to be alone and reflect on what he meant to me. (Courtesy of *Sporting News* via Getty Images)

Bernie Williams was one of my all-time favorite teammates. We spent a lot of time together in the outfield, in the dugout, in the clubhouse, and even when Bernie played the guitar and I played the drums. We all wish we could be as multitalented and cool as Bernie. (Courtesy of Jamie Squire/Allsport via Getty Images)

Joe Girardi was one of my closest friends in baseball. Even after we retired and Joe was managing the Yankees and I was announcing games for the YES Network, we remained very close and always found time to talk about baseball and our families. (Courtesy of Jim McIsaac/Getty Images)

I was a passionate player, and I never hesitated to tell an umpire when I thought he had missed a call. That's what happened with Jerry Crawford during Game 5 of the 2000 World Series against the Mets. Lee Mazzilli, our first base coach, tried to calm me down. (Courtesy of Stan Honda/AFP via Getty Images)

During my final game at Yankee Stadium in the 2001 World Series, the fans repeatedly chanted my name, even as we were losing to the Diamondbacks. It was an unbelievably classy gesture from the best fans in baseball. As I ran off the field late in the game, I was choked up with emotion. (Courtesy of *Sporting News* via Getty Images)

Andy Pettitte and I were friends, teammates, and neighbors in New York, sharing many special memories with each other and our families. Unfortunately, this isn't one of those special memories. That's a glum Andy and an unhappy me in the dugout during Game 6 of the 2001 World Series. We lost to the Diamondbacks 15-2. (Courtesy of Jeff Gross/Allsport via Getty Images)

I was incredibly honored when the Yankees dedicated a plaque to me in Monument Park in 2014. I never imagined being remembered in such a wonderful way. In this picture, I'm surrounded by some of the men who helped me along that journey. From left to right, it's Joe Torre, Gene Michael, Gene Monahan, me, Mariano Rivera, Tino Martinez, David Cone, and Jorge Posada. Great teammates and great friends. (Courtesy of Getty Images)

Jeter just said "O'Neill!" because he never called me Paul, and then he shook his head and laughed. If the old man didn't know what Smith's song was about, Jeter wasn't going to help me. Wherever Jeter was away from the field, Posada was always nearby. They were very close friends from their minor-league days, and that bond strengthened in the majors.

If I had to pick one player to define the toughness of some of our Yankee teams, I would pick Jorge. I loved the way he played. So passionate. So intense. So driven to succeed. If Posada felt like a player needed to be scolded, he never hesitated to get in someone's face. Not every player wants to do that or can do that, but Jorge was a leader and he had the respect of everyone in our clubhouse.

Team meetings weren't limited to one voice with Torre, as he wanted input from his players. Jorge was very vocal and always said, "We're going to grind." That meant we were going to work as hard as we possibly could and find a way to win. That was grinding. Jorge said it so often that Torre essentially adopted it as a way to end some meetings.

"Jorge," Torre would say, "what are we going to do?"

A very confident Posada would shout, "We're going to grind!"

In some ways, that might seem trite or like it was a joke. But it wasn't. That exchange meant something to us. It's who Jorge was and it's who we were.

Before Jorge became the full-time catcher, the Yankees were fortunate to have Joe Girardi behind the plate. Joe was a selfless player and a smart player, and that was evident in the way he called games and in the way he helped pitchers make in-game adjustments. Joe was more interested in the way pitchers pitched than in the way he hit.

There would be games when Joe was hitless and didn't love his swings, but he would be ecstatic in postgame interviews because Cone had pitched superbly with a bunch of strikeouts. Not every catcher is like that. They might say they are, but players want to succeed individually, too. Joe tethered himself to his pitchers so their success was also his success.

Joe and I had a strong relationship and I would describe him as one of my true friends. I was teammates with dozens of players in my seventeen-year career, and I called a lot of them friends. But only a handful of those teammates were true friends who knew my family well and who shared experiences with me away from the field. I was fortunate that Joe, who tried to recruit me to be his hitting coach when he managed the Marlins, was one of those people.

So was Chris Sabo, another good buddy and my teammate with the Cincinnati Reds. We called him "Spuds" because he resembled Spuds MacKenzie, the dog from the old beer commercials. I admired Spuds for his mental toughness, and I learned a lot from watching how he dealt with adversity on the field. He was a slick-fielding third baseman and a tough dude, a tough dude who hit .563 during the 1990 World Series and landed on the cover of *Sports Illustrated*.

Andy Pettitte was also on my list of true, lifelong friends. Proximity helped Andy and me become unbelievable friends. He lived next door to me when we played for the Yankees and we used to drive to the games together. Our wives were friends, our kids were friends, and we all enjoyed that closeness. Andy and I had a lot of fulfilling discussions on those rides to and from the Stadium, always trying to be good listeners and always trying to lift each other up.

When baseball was on hiatus for a week after the unfathomable terrorist attacks of 9/11, Andy wanted to play catch to keep his arm in shape. We met in our backyards and tossed the ball back and forth. I couldn't believe how heavy his ball was and how much movement he was generating on his sinker and his cutter. I was a major-league player and I was having trouble snatching some of his pitches because the ball was moving so much. And we were just playing catch. This wasn't a bullpen session. I kept moving farther away from Andy because I didn't want one of his pitches to clip me on the wrist.

With nineteen postseason wins, Andy was a big-game pitcher. I would say the exact same thing about Cone, who loved being a hired gun and who might know more about pitching than anyone I've ever met. I would describe Coney as the perfect blend of talent, intelligence, creativity, and tenacity. When Coney lowered his arm angle and dropped down to throw a slider, he flustered right-handed hitters. Very few pitchers have the confidence or the guts to change arm angles like that, but Cone did it as casually as if he was playing Wiffle ball. Coney won a Cy Young Award with the Kansas City Royals and five World Series titles (four with the Yankees and one with the Blue Jays), and he always performed as if every pitch determined if he could take his next breath.

I had some success against Coney in my career, but he was so intriguing because he was the type of pitcher who was thinking two and three pitches ahead to try and stifle batters. Quite often, Coney would start me out by throwing pitches on the outside part of the plate. He knew I liked to extend my arms and try to hit those pitches the opposite way, but he tried to throw pitches a bit outside to get me to chase. If he got ahead in the count, Coney would bounce a slider off my back foot or maybe try to sneak a fastball or two inside.

Now that we share a broadcast booth for the YES Network, I get to listen to him analyze pitchers every night. He still talks like a pitcher who is sweating about the next full count, and I learn something new from him during every game. As impressed as I was with Coney when we were teammates and opponents, I'm just as impressed with the pitching insight he offers on TV. The dude is a pitching genius.

The man who had a perfect position to watch Cone throw sliders and splitters was Tino Martinez, our first baseman. Like Jeter, Posada, Pettitte, Cone, Girardi, and many others, Tino was another player whose primary focus was the team. Yes, Tino was intense and he wanted to succeed as a hitter, but he was a team-oriented player.

Before games, Tino and I would discuss the left-handed relievers that we were both likely to see. Tino was more of a pull hitter, and he was a much better power hitter, so teams would pitch him differently than me. But it was still helpful to discuss the way pitchers were approaching and attacking him. If I noticed something about the way a slider broke or a certain sequence the pitcher liked, I would share the information with Tino. And he would do the same.

What was sometimes amusing about our chats is that Tino

and I couldn't always explain why he had succeeded against a certain pitcher and I had not or vice versa. And sometimes, we'd share our frustration when we talked about trying to hit against a funky lefty like Paul Assenmacher. Including the postseason, I was 5 for 32 with 1 homer and twelve strikeouts off Assenmacher, while Tino was 4 for 19 with no homers and four strikeouts. Although I homered off Assenmacher in the 1997 playoffs, neither of us found much of a solution for him.

Bernie would join in our conversations, too, but as a switch-hitter, he was in a more favorable position because he never had to face a breaking pitch that was coming at him. Like Posada, another switch-hitter, Bernie avoided that type of uncomfortable at bat. I'm so dependent on my left hand that I can barely use my right hand to spoon some soup out of a bowl, and that's why I have such respect for players who hit from both sides of the plate.

As I trudged across the same area of right field in game after game, I would inevitably create a barren patch of grass. It wasn't too large, but it was noticeable. As a joke, I would point to the spotty patch and tell Bernie that I would cover that tiny area defensively and he had to handle everything else in right, right-center, and center. The agreeable Bernie would tip his cap and laugh.

If I had to pick an "All–Nice Guy" team from my years as a player, Scott Brosius would be on that club. After Brosius's average dropped from .304 in 1996 to .203 in the following season, the Yankees acquired him from the Oakland A's in November 1997 and he proved to be a terrific addition. Brosius had a tremendous bounce-back season with us, hitting

.300 with 19 homers and 98 runs batted in while playing slick defense at third base.

Armed with a dry sense of humor, Brosius would mock the idea that he was on the verge of knocking in 100 runs and he was routinely batting eighth or ninth. Bro didn't mind hitting in the bottom of our powerhouse lineup and didn't think Torre should elevate him, but he amused us by joking about it. Everyone was rooting for Brosius to reach offensive milestones like the .300 average and those 100 RBIs because he was such a likable guy. We were all thrilled when he won the Most Valuable Player Award for the 1998 World Series after hitting .471 with 2 homers against the Padres.

When 1999 started, everyone wondered if the mighty Yankees could match our incredible 1998. I wasn't sure any team could be as powerful or as blessed as the 1998 team, but I thought we could win another title. We still had the same core players and we also made a blockbuster deal to acquire Roger Clemens from the Blue Jays for David Wells, Graeme Lloyd, and Homer Bush. One of the best teams of all time added one of the best pitchers of all time, which was a massive sign that the front office wasn't resting on what we accomplished a year earlier.

Three weeks before the season started, we were reminded that baseball players aren't immune to frightening medical diagnoses, as we learned that Torre had prostate cancer. Torre called me, Girardi, and Cone into his office and told us the news. We were all stunned and saddened. Joe asked us to tell the rest of the players about his condition. We were worried about our leader, the man who had done so much for all of us. But Joe was hopeful the cancer had been detected early.

As much as I adored Zimmer, our bench coach and the interim manager, it was weird to not have Joe around. He was such a calming force in the dugout and off the field, too. Once the games start, players must focus and we all did. But Joe's absence left a void in a team that relied on him.

I still remember when Torre returned to the dugout in Fenway Park in late May. We weren't expecting him back on that specific day, and all of a sudden, there he was. Same sleepy eyes. Same supportive voice. Same chipper attitude. It was like one of our long-lost friends had returned. Everything felt right again. When Joe brought the lineup card out before the game, the Red Sox fans were classy and gave him a warm and extended ovation. The message on the scoreboard read, "Welcome Back." We lost that night, but we had our manager back.

As our season cruised along, I was delighted to be part of another monumental game on July 18, 1999. More than monumental, it was perfect. Cone, my friend and someone I deeply respected for his ferocious competitiveness, pitched a perfect game against the Montreal Expos at the Stadium. Coney did it on Yogi Berra Day while throwing 88 pitches. Yogi, of course, wore number 8 with the Yankees.

It was a bright and sweltering afternoon and it's not always easy to pick up the ball in those conditions. The glare was an early factor as Terry Jones, the second batter of the game, hit a tumbling liner to right field. The ball was sinking fast, but I charged forward and knew I would have to slide to try to make the play. I sprawled across the grass and caught the ball about waist-high. Coney was actually heading to back up third because he thought Jones's ball was an extra-base hit. It was only the second out and seemed uneventful, but it proved to be a significant early play, as Coney kept throwing slider after slider and baffling the Expos. As a hitter, I knew how Coney's slider would spin and drop, and on that day, he featured the best slider he'd ever thrown. It was a pitch that made a drastic left turn as it reached the plate. I was thrilled for Coney and thrilled for us, as the perfect game was another part of a magical year.

Any semblance of personal magic expired on October 2, the day I tried to corral a fly ball against Tampa Bay and collided with a low right-field wall at Tropicana Field. It was a painful and vicious collision, as I fractured my tenth rib on the right side. I had internal bleeding, which prevented me from getting a cortisone shot to dull the pain. The postseason was a few days away and I knew it was going to be a struggle to play.

At least I could still laugh without hurting myself too much. And I did laugh on the final day of the season, because Torre handed me the managing duties since our game was meaningless in the standings. My first move as manager was to dismiss Zimmer as bench coach as payback for all the times he teased me when I was griping in the dugout. I made Girardi my bench coach. Well, we lost the game 6-2, proving I was a better hitter than a manager. I actually didn't end up managing the entire game because I needed to get medical treatment for my ribs.

Could I handle the pain and still be productive? That was the persistent question about me that October. And as I was dealing with my physical pain, my family was dealing with an avalanche of emotional pain, as my father was experiencing serious heart problems at Lenox Hill Hospital in New York.

My world changed forever at 3:00 a.m. on October 27. That's when I received the call that Charles "Chick" O'Neill, my hero, died of complications from heart disease at the age of seventy-nine. Anything I ever accomplished in my life was because of the dedication of my parents, making that an agonizing and excruciating day. I couldn't digest the fact that I'd never have another conversation with Dad or hear him say, "I love that swing. That's another great line drive." I couldn't comprehend how lonely my mother would be.

As distraught and depressed as I was, there was no doubt that I was going to play in a potential clinching Game 4 of the World Series that night. In my mind and with my beliefs, I trusted that my dad would be watching and that he would be pain-free. I had to play. I appreciate that Torre offered me the opportunity to do what was best for me. But as a baseball lifer who owed everything to his dad, the best thing for me was to play. I wept in the clubhouse that day while receiving unforgettable support from Torre and my teammates, including Brosius and Luis Sojo. Both had recently lost their dads, too.

With Clemens pitching powerfully into the eighth, we stopped the Braves 4-1 to sweep the series and win another title. After the final out, I was an emotional mess. My eyes were glassy as I robotically hugged my teammates near the mound. Torre wrapped his hands around my neck and pulled me close. We were both crying. At one point, I hugged reliever Mike Stanton and started to collapse. I was so drained that

I couldn't stand. As the on-field celebration continued, I ran into the dugout while wiping tears from my eyes. I was elated we won, but I was filled with too much sadness to celebrate. The man I called "Old-Timer" and "Little Buddy" was gone. My world would never be the same.

— ⊂⊃ —

Baseball, like time, marches on. The off-season was different and difficult for my family, but as the new year dawned, I was eager to get back to a routine and to return to spring training for the 2000 season. Obviously, we wanted to win another title and become the first team since the Oakland A's in 1972, 1973, and 1974 to win three straight championships.

Every time someone asks me to rate my World Series titles with the Yankees, I sigh and tell them it's like asking me to rate my three children. I would never pick Aaron over Andy or Andy over Allie or Allie over Aaron because I love them equally. Just like I would never pick 1996 over 1998 or 1999 or 2000. I cherish all of those championships equally. But in terms of endless drama, constant excitement, overwhelming hype, and a local rivalry playing out on a national stage, the 2000 World Series against the Mets was a special event.

I just wish I was hitting better at the time. Even though I drove in 100 runs for the fourth straight season, I was troubled by a hip injury and experienced a dismal September. That lack of production led to Joe pinch-hitting for me twice during the American League Championship Series. With the bases loaded in Game 5, I was already in the batter's box when I was called back to the dugout so Glenallen Hill, a righty batter, could pinch-hit against lefty Arthur Rhodes. I wasn't thrilled about being lifted and I definitely wasn't thrilled about being removed in such a haphazard manner. Afterward, I held my thumb and index finger an inch apart and told reporters, "I felt about this big." Still, I responded with 2 hits and 3 runs batted in as we prevailed in Game 6 and earned a spot in the World Series.

And I was back in the lineup for Game 1 of the World Series, a game we were fortunate to win over the Mets. I've already detailed how helpless I felt in my 10-pitch at bat against Armando Benítez and how my walk helped us tie the game in the ninth and eventually win it in twelve innings. Who knows what might have happened in that series if we lost the opener? More than two decades later, I'm going to finally reveal what else helped me in that series. Let's call it the magic of Yogi.

I'm convinced that one of the reasons I had a solid game with one hit and two walks was because Yogi stopped by my locker before the game, picked up my bats, rubbed them, and said, "I'm putting some hits in these bats." The idea of the legendary Berra offering me some luck during the World Series was much needed juju, since I had ended the regular season with 4 hits in 39 at bats. There was no one like the lovable Yogi in the Yankee world. So kind, so funny, and so happy to be talking baseball. He had ten World Series rings. Ten! The playful Yogi would often amble over to Jeter's locker and tease Jeter about how he'd never match Yogi in the jewelry department. Yogi was right. Jeter finished with five World Series rings.

But let's get back to my bats. Unsolicited, Yogi, the man who had a ring for every finger, took the same meaty hands that had once caught Don Larsen's perfect game in the World Series and rubbed my bats. A few hours later, I reached base three times in our win.

Amped up when I arrived at the ballpark the next day, I kept asking everyone, "Is Yogi here yet?" I wasn't the most superstitious guy, but I became superstitious about Berra and my bats. Was it good luck or good karma or nothing? I don't know, but I wanted it to keep going. Let me put it this way: if I had found out Yogi wasn't coming to the game, I would have driven my bats to his house in New Jersey for more caressing. Players get crazy about these things, especially in crucial games.

Earlier in my career, I was superstitious enough to sleep with my bat under my mattress. I was in a deep slump, and Ron Oester, my Reds teammate, told me I should place my game-used bat between the mattress and the box spring to change my luck. I felt so lost at the plate that I tried it. And it worked! I immediately started to sting the baseball after my bat traveled from the dugout to the bedroom. So, of course, I was on a mission to find Yogi.

Eventually, Yogi arrived and I almost tackled him and dragged him over to work his magic on my bats again. And I had three hits in Game 2, including two after Mike Hampton walked Posada ahead of me. And then I socked three more hits in Game 3! After not having back-to-back three-hit games all season, I did it against the Mets. I also laced two triples during that series, two more than I had all season.

Yogi was incredibly knowledgeable about life and baseball, but he was also the most humble superstar I've ever met.

When it came to hitting, Yogi could explain the level of confidence he had as a hitter and could explain how and why he would succeed. But we didn't have technical conversations about hitting, like the ones I had with Ted Williams and like the many conversations I had with Don Mattingly.

Since Yogi was a free swinger and one of the best bad-ball hitters in baseball history, we had dramatically different approaches. I hunted for strikes and didn't want to swing at pitches outside of the zone. Meanwhile, Yogi was such a confident hitter that he would swing at ankle-high pitches or shoulder-high pitches and still make solid contact. The three-time MVP was a power hitter and had 358 homers and a mere 414 strikeouts in his Hall of Fame career. I wish I had Yogi's uncanny skills, but I didn't. If I left the zone, I was in trouble.

When it came to discussing his approach to World Series games, Yogi was a great resource because he treated the games like he was still a kid. He didn't allow World Series games to be any bigger than any other games and he didn't let the moment get too big, which is the hallmark of a great player. And he was a great player.

If you don't believe in the magic of Yogi, here are some statistics. Heading into the 2000 World Series, I was 9 for 39 in the first two rounds of the playoffs. After Yogi rubbed my bats, I went 9 for 19 against the Mets. Coincidence? Probably not. I think Yogi's actions surprised me and made me laugh and that relaxed me during a tense time, and a calm confidence carried over for me at the plate.

A couple of hours after we won the 2000 World Series in five games, I was in my own world as I walked through the corridors of Shea Stadium to get to our team bus. I was thrilled and tired—really tired. Along my three-minute walk to the parking lot, I was intercepted by a reporter: "How much," he asked, "have you been thinking about your dad?"

With my eyes trained on the concrete floor, I answered the reporter by showing him that I had two gold wedding bands on my finger. My own thick band was on my ring finger and a thinner band, my father's band, was resting above it. My mother had given it to me two days earlier and I immediately put it on my finger. That ring reminded me of my dad and made me feel closer to him. I still wear it today. It had been a year since my father died, so I thanked the reporter for remembering to ask about my dad. "I'd much rather talk about my father than about what has changed for me at the plate," I said. "He was my hero."

I was more than content after 2000 because we had won our third straight title, but also because I was able to enjoy the ride. I hadn't enjoyed the 1999 postseason because of my father's worsening health and his eventual passing. When I think of 1999, my dad's death overshadows everything else. I can recite what I did in all of my postseason at bats except 1999. That postseason is a blur.

As a father myself, I always tried to emulate my dad by making decisions that best suited my family. So, even as I felt content, I also knew it was time to make the poignant admission that my career was coming to an end. I knew 2001 would be the last time I wore a Yankees uniform. And trust me, I also knew I wasn't going to spend the entire season talking about my impending retirement.

CHAPTER 9

A Final Bronx Tale

I didn't want to have an endless going-away party. I didn't want to talk about retirement every day when the Yankees were trying to win games and win another title. I just wanted to play baseball for one more year, like I had always done, and go home. That was my plan for 2001 and I was stubborn about adhering to it.

My dad was my greatest role model and he was a humble, quiet man, a man who didn't brag about having a nice car or a spacious house. He believed in doing your work, doing it well, and then returning and doing the same thing the next day. If one of your colleagues or friends wanted to praise you, that was fine. But don't even spend a minute telling the world how great you are. The world will draw its own conclusions.

Anyone who ever saw me hit one of my 281 career homers watched me connect with the pitch, turn my head to the right, drop the bat to the ground, and run around the bases without any flair or any flexing. That was my modest approach and that came from watching the way my dad behaved for his whole life.

Charles O'Neill was pursuing a baseball career when, like so many other heroic and young Americans, he left for World War II and became a paratrooper. After an injury, he returned and pitched in the minor leagues. While Dad never reached the majors, he wouldn't have dreamed of complaining about enduring a military interruption to his career. Dad came from a generation that didn't grouse or gloat. We were taught to be respectful and unpretentious, just like my parents.

With my father's words and actions always fresh in my mind, I was adamant about not having our season include a "Goodbye to the Warrior" tour. It would have made me uncomfortable to have the spotlight on me. And I planned to be as ornery and disciplined as I needed to be to make sure that kind of narrative didn't happen.

In subsequent seasons, I watched Derek Jeter and Mariano Rivera, my former Yankees teammates, have wonderful good-bye seasons in which they were celebrated with countless ovations and creative gifts. Those love affairs were tremendous and deserving because they were both legends and were both first-ballot Hall of Famers.

I'm a Midwestern guy who, despite my many outbursts on the field and my skirmishes with umpires, is actually kind of reserved. Don't laugh! I really am. I was traded to New York and found a second home, and I loved every minute of being an adopted New Yorker and winning four championships there. My nine seasons in New York were the greatest nine seasons of my life. But I didn't want to be the center of attention in my final year, and honestly, I didn't think I deserved it. Even my dad, my biggest fan, would have told me that.

Two weeks after we won the 2000 World Series, I signed a one-year contract with the Yankees and said, "My plans are, right now, this is my last year. I want to have a great year and go to the World Series again." We had a chance to win four straight championships, which hadn't been accomplished since the Yankees won five in a row from 1949 to 1953. I was thrilled to have the opportunity to finish my career with many of the same men who had won the last three in a row—linchpin players like Jeter, Rivera, Martinez, Williams, Pettitte, Brosius, and Knoblauch. That was my focus and I wanted that to be everyone else's focus.

The cool and superb Jeter was the face of our franchise and he had signed a ten-year, $189 million contract in the off-season, so, as always and as expected, he received an avalanche of media attention. We had signed Mike Mussina, the smart, competitive right-hander from the division-rival Orioles, to a six-year, $88.5 million deal, so his adjustment to New York was also extensively covered. With those two stars and our pursuit of a fourth straight title accruing a lot of headlines, I hoped to be the thirty-eight-year-old guy who quietly squeezed in one more year.

On my first day of spring training, I playfully and seriously begged a reporter not to turn my last season into a fare-well tour. I mentioned that I "didn't want to talk about this being my last spring training, my last Opening Day, my thirteenth-to-the-last Friday." Yeah, I had that line about the thirteenth-to-the-last Friday cued up.

About as close as I came to reiterating it was my final year was when I talked about coaching my son Aaron's second-grade basketball team in Cincinnati. We were called the Aviators and we didn't fly too high. In fact, we were awful and the coach should be blamed. We had more air balls than field goals. We played thirteen games. We lost twelve of them.

"If the kids go 1-12," I said, "you better spend a little more time with them."

Hint, hint. It was time for me to go home and be with my family. My three kids deserved to have a full school year in Ohio, not shuttling between schools in Florida, New York, and Cincinnati, depending on whether it was spring training, the baseball season, or the off-season.

Plus, when Nevalee and I spoke about what the Yankees had accomplished since the midnineties, it just felt like it was the right time to retire. I spent my whole career grinding for more and trying to win. Chasing hits. Chasing a .300 average. Chasing 100 runs batted in. Most of all, I was chasing championships. And in 2001, I didn't feel as if I was chasing anything anymore. Obviously, I wanted us to win it all one last time, but I knew I was running the last lap of my chase.

To get acclimated in the early days of spring, I wouldn't swing a bat too forcefully and I would only hit in the indoor cage. My goal was to build up some calluses on my hands before I even thought about facing any high velocity pitches. During the last half of my career, I never picked up a bat in the winter, so I took a methodical approach to getting ready in Florida. I lifted weights, played tennis, and worked out to stay in shape in the off-season, but I waited until spring training to develop my leg kick and get my swing to a comfortable place. It was a gradual way to ease back into hitting, as I couldn't take a few months off and then automatically start crushing fastballs, which I once proved to myself in a painful way.

On a random, chilly afternoon in Cincinnati, I was hanging out with my brother Robert and a few friends at a sports complex that featured some batting machines. Everyone implored me to get into the cage and hit against 90-mile-per-hour fastballs. None of them could connect against that velocity so they wanted the only big leaguer in the bunch to show them how easy it was. Easy? Really? I didn't want to do it, but I bowed to peer pressure and selected a bat.

We inserted some coins and the old Iron Mike pitching machine fired the first fastball, and the 90-mile-per-hour pitch felt like 110. Was Nolan Ryan hiding inside this machine? I was uncomfortable because I hadn't faced live pitching in a while. All I wanted to do was smack a few line drives, satisfy the restless group, and complete the round. This might sound silly, but I felt pressure to produce for this audience.

After tracking a few pitches, I was finally ready to swing. Or at least I thought I was. I swung so late that the baseball ricocheted off a nearby pole and bounced back and hit me in a spot where no man wants to be hit. It drilled me in the groin. I tumbled to the concrete floor, writhing in pain. But the machine never stopped pumping 90-mile-per-hour bullets right over my head! I was in a lot of pain in a sensitive area and I was trying to avoid getting plunked in the noggin with another pitch. It was the equivalent of a bad *Saturday Night Live* skit. Everyone was laughing except me. Thankfully, there's no video of this incident.

That was an embarrassing display, and as humorous as it was, that incident stayed with me through the years and reminded me not to do anything to embarrass myself. In a strange way, it contributed to me developing a mantra I used before the 2001 season: "Don't embarrass yourself in your final season." In addition to telling myself that, I also stressed the importance of hitting on top of the baseball, hitting it hard, and driving through it. I used those commands every day and they worked.

For the hundredth time, I must repeat I was a line-drive hitter and not a home-run hitter. But I was hitting a respectable .279 and had socked 8 homers in the first twenty games of the season, something I had never done before. My previous high for homers through the first twenty games had been 6 in 1994, when I also had a robust .443 average. Still, as I was walking out the door toward retirement, I was also exiting with a bit of a bang.

The most comical homer came against the Red Sox at Yankee Stadium, and it was funny because of my frustrated reaction. We were trailing 3-2 in the bottom of the tenth inning when Derek Lowe, who had a vicious sinker, hung a 1-2 curveball. My eyes widened, I took a mighty swing, and I *thought* I got under the ball and failed to hit it deep enough. My shoulders sagged like I had been defeated, I twisted my head in disgust, I looked up to the blue skies, and I slammed my bat to the dirt. Dejectedly, I trotted toward first.

As I jogged down the line, I noticed right fielder Darren Lewis backpedaling toward the fence and getting ready to leap and catch the ball. Shockingly, to me, he never jumped. And then I realized the ball had cleared the fence and landed in the first two rows, making me the hitter who threw a tantrum about an actual home run.

I should have been elated because I had tied the game. And I was. But I also felt sheepish because of my angry reaction. When I crossed home, I gave limp high fives to my teammates. I was still trying to figure out how I had misjudged a shot that I thought would travel 313 feet, at best. Of course, Don Zimmer, the bench coach who loved to agitate me, laughed as heartily as if he'd witnessed a classic set from Rodney Dangerfield. Soon after my own comedy routine, David Justice belted a game-winning homer off Lowe, so we all laughed—a lot of it at my expense.

To be a successful hitter, I needed to be focused and driven to succeed every day. I was never the type of hitter who could have one incredible month and have that production carry me for half the season. I was a day-after-day performer, a player who was at his best when he did something to help a team every day. It wasn't like I could say, "Hey, guys. I stink this week. I'll help out next week." I judged myself on producing every day. *Every day.*

But at the age of thirty-eight, I noticed it was more difficult to concentrate for every pitch of every at bat. That was alarming and unnerving to me. I was a laser-focused hitter, chanting to myself before every pitch, and believing, really believing, I could get a hit every time I was in the batter's box. Being relentless on every pitch is what made me a solid hitter, because I simply refused to be an easy out. "Obviously, he doesn't like to get out, ever," Jeter once said about me.

Slowly and frustratingly, my mind would sometimes wander at the plate in my final season. I wasn't tired or disinterested, but my concentration wasn't as sharp as it had been and I couldn't control it. With age, our vision and our reflexes will wane and we can't stop that process, no matter how much we try.

Troubled by this development, I discussed it with Manager Joe Torre, and he explained how concentration issues impact many professional athletes. Torre cited golfers who fizzle on the third or fourth day of a tournament because their mental focus fades. It would seem easy for a hitter to remain alert and ready for 4 at bats a night. But if I had a 10-pitch at bat like the one I had against Armando Benítez in the 2000 World Series, I wasn't always able to fully engage. And if a hitter loses his clarity on one pitch, it's over. That will be the last pitch of the at bat. And that reality drove me absolutely crazy.

No matter how many pregame swings I took, how much video I watched, or how many times I spoke to myself, I sometimes had a lost moment on a pitch. I was fired up for my last season, so enthusiasm wasn't a problem. It was just the inability to be locked-in for every single pitch. Even thinking about it now annoys the heck out of me.

"When you get older, the work part of it is getting yourself to where you need to be just to have an at bat," Torre said. "There's no question it's harder to hit as you get older. You're standing up there and it's not like, 'Where am I?' It's more like, 'Where is it?' Because if you're locked-in as a hitter, you're not going to miss anything."

And because Joe was Joe and he was a great storyteller, he recounted a story about his concentration that involved Bob Gibson. When Joe was playing with the Cardinals against the San Francisco Giants at Candlestick Park, he noticed a white truck parked behind the outfield fence. As Joe was searching for the spin on a white baseball, he didn't want the white truck to inter-fere with his line of vision, so he asked the umpire to have the truck moved. The ump obliged. "Bob Gibson teased me about that whole thing and said, 'You see everything,'" Joe recalled. "But the thing is, when you're really concentrating and you're locked-in, you do see everything. That's where a hitter wants to be."

I can't specify how often my concentration lapsed, because it was sporadic. For a week or two, I would see every pitch and react to every pitch and not experience any lapses. But then I'd have a few games where I couldn't remain honed in on every pitch. Maybe it happened because of a shabby swing, an inconsistent strike zone, a slow-working pitcher, or some other distraction. Things just weren't as seamless as they should have been.

How can a player show up for a major-league game and not simply be able to concentrate? I wish I had the answer. I could have used that answer in 2001. Instead, I learned that, for me, there was a big difference between being a thirty-seven-year-old player and a thirty-eight-year-old player. I'd never forfeited at bats the way I lost them that season.

After studying Don Mattingly and Wade Boggs and notic-ing how they never relented and never took pitches off, the notion that I was losing my edge and giving away at bats wasn't easy to digest. I talked hitting with Mattingly as much or more than any hitter I ever played with, but I also had beneficial discussions with Boggs.

Boggs's intensity in every at bat was breathtaking, as he treated every pitch like it was in a deciding World Series game. That might sound like hyperbole, but it's not. As a Hall-of-Fame hitter, Boggs had a determined approach and he stuck with that approach. He was the same hitter on every single pitch and every single at bat, even saying his swing had not changed since he was a Little Leaguer. Obviously, he was a fantastic hitter. But to get to that point, Boggs had to be intent on what he was doing as a hitter. He stood close to the plate and wouldn't give pitchers an inch on the inside corner as he tried to hit the ball the other way.

If Boggs wasn't ripping hits the opposite way, he was fouling pitches off to keep an at bat alive, he was making a pitcher work even harder, or he was watching poor pitches sail out of the strike zone. After observing Boggs every day, it was simple to understand how and why he pieced together those seasons of hitting .350 and .360 and won five batting titles. I felt blessed to win one.

When I watched Boggs's competitiveness and fearlessness in every at bat, that rubbed off on me. It was learning through osmosis, like Pete Rose advised me to do when I debuted with the Reds in 1985. I had already been an All-Star and a World Series champ by the time I became teammates with Boggs, but he and Donnie helped remind me of the importance of every pitch. And that's why some of my at bats in 2001 were so exasperating.

Despite my occasional lapses in concentration, I had a solid year and became the oldest player to ever have a 20-20 season, with 21 homers and 22 stolen bases. I also had a slash line of .267/.330/.459 and drove in 70 runs. But that season was a grind in fighting through this focus issue.

Because I was so consumed with my at bats and with us making the playoffs, I didn't allow myself to think about too many "lasts" until the final month of the season. Oddly enough, one of the first times I thought deeply about my retirement was when I sat in the third-base dugout at Fenway Park on September 2, for what I figured would be my last game there. It was a few hours before the first pitch, so the stadium was mostly empty and comfortably quiet.

Even though I was the enemy in Boston, I enjoyed playing in that cozy, noisy, and ancient ballpark. Fenway was born in 1912, meaning I stood in the same right field as Babe Ruth and so many other legends. As I sat by myself, I realized how fortunate I was to be part of the fierce Yankees–Red Sox rivalry. Every game was special.

That night, I went 0 for 3 in my Boston finale, but I was almost a small part of history. Again. Mussina was impeccable in retiring the first 26 batters of the game and was within one strike of pitching a perfect game. But Carl Everett whacked a two-strike fastball to left to destroy Mussina's bid for perfection. He finished with a one-hitter in a 1-0 victory, a bittersweet win.

On the brief flight from Boston to New York, I sat next to Mussina and I didn't know what to say. I didn't have any inspirational or consoling words. It was the only season we were teammates, but he was one of the smartest, if not the smartest guy, in our clubhouse. I could tell he was numb and mentally drained. Coming that close to perfection was agonizing and was going to irk him for a long, long time. We talked, but we didn't talk about his near miss.

Injuries are a part of being a major-league player, especially since we play 162 games in six months. If you want to be a competitor and you want to help your team win, you have to play through some injuries. I played with fractured ribs, a hip injury, a strained hamstring, and other nicks and bruises during some of our postseason runs because there was no way I was going to miss those games.

But in 2001, I noticed the minor injuries I used to just deal with didn't feel as minor anymore. Again, I would get worn down physically and mentally and I wasn't able to bounce back the way I did when I was twenty-five. It's not an easy thing to admit because we all want to play forever, but it happens. After games, I still dutifully lifted weights three times a week to fight Father Time. Somehow, I played in 133 of our first 141 games.

And there was a different challenge every night. It was always a challenge to oppose the talented Pedro Martínez because he was so competitive and he had so many ways to make hitters look silly. He didn't seem to be his overpowering self on September 7, but I was still content when I laced a 3-2 change-up for a run-scoring single. When Alfonso Soriano followed with a single to shallow center, I hustled 180 feet to third. I eventually scored on an infield error. There was nothing different about my dash around the bases against Boston.

But as I trotted to play right field for the next inning, I felt a painful sensation in my left foot. I knew something was wrong and that was weird, because all I had done was sprint from first to third. The discomfort was so intense that I yelled to center fielder Bernie Williams to take any shots to right-center because I couldn't run at full speed.

I rested the foot, but the pain persisted and an MRI revealed

I had a stress fracture. I was flabbergasted. It was crazy to me that I had hurt myself by just running the bases, which I had done a few hundred times that season. I asked myself, "Why now?" I play baseball every day, and now I'm getting a stress fracture because I ran the bases? I just wanted to scream, "Are you bleeping kidding me?"

While my teammates prepared for our game against the Red Sox on September 9, I glumly walked around the clubhouse wearing a protective boot. I couldn't run or put weight on my foot. With about three weeks left in the regular season, I didn't need a calendar to remind me I might have a difficult time being ready for October. My mind was cloudy as I drove home that night, exasperated by this unbelievable foot fiasco.

A couple days later, I woke up and went to the gym to free my mind from worrying about the foot injury. "Just keep working out so you will be ready for the postseason," I preached to myself. Between exercises, I glanced up at a TV and saw the most horrible images as an airplane crashed into one of the towers at the World Trade Center. I stayed glued to the TV for any explanation about this tragedy. Less than twenty minutes later, a second plane rammed into the second tower. The news reports were saying this was a terrorist attack.

Like everyone else, I was numb with worry. I was worried about my wife and kids, worried about our friends and family, and worried about everyone who had been impacted by these devastating actions. The terrorists also crashed a plane into the Pentagon and a fourth plane went down in Shanksville, Pennsylvania.

We picked up our kids from school and tried to protect them from the hysteria and fear that were all around us. At night, we took a ride to get ice cream just to give us something to do. I remember driving past candlelight vigils and wondering how many of those people had friends or relatives who were missing.

Everyone was in a state of shock and we didn't know where to go or what to do. My life revolves around baseball, and baseball wasn't even occupying one minute of my thoughts at that time. I was thinking about the thousands of lives that were taken and how our world had changed. Nothing else mattered.

Obviously, our season was paused as our country dealt with the worst terrorist attack in our history. Like everyone else, I felt scared and helpless. I've never been good at sitting still and doing nothing. In such a desperate and depressing time, I wanted to feel useful. I wanted to do something.

Four days later, I was part of a group of thirteen players and coaches who ventured into Manhattan to visit the Javits Center, St. Vincent's Hospital, and the 69th Regiment Armory. The Armory was the venue where people had gathered with pictures and DNA samples in hopes of finding information about their lost and presumably deceased loved ones. It was emotional and heart-wrenching to meet with people who were hoping and praying for a speck of information and a miracle reunion. What can you possibly say to bring them any relief?

A young boy, who was five or six years old, recognized me

and asked me to sign his Beanie Baby. I signed it and spoke to him for a while. When he saw I was wearing a walking boot, he said, "I hope you feel better soon." I had to hold back tears. Can you imagine that? He had just lost one of his parents and he was telling me that he hoped I felt better. Talk about strength and bravery.

Every person I met had a story. A story about their dad, their mom, their spouse, their sibling, or their child. And they had Yankees stories, too. So, I listened. I was hesitant and almost embarrassed to think the Yankees or baseball would have any relevance, with all of the unimaginable sadness these people were experiencing. But all of a sudden, I would see a smile on someone's face because they loved the Yankees, and it emphasized how important it was to simply be there. By being there, I guess we allowed some people to share a baseball bond with the folks they had lost. Believe me, after visiting with the grieving people that day, I walked away from them a changed person.

In everything the Yankees did for the remainder of the season, the specter of 9/11 hovered over us. New York was traumatized—terribly traumatized. We all wanted to win for ourselves and our place in history, but we wanted to give back to New York, too. After all that misery and sadness, we could give Yankee fans three hours of entertainment each night, and hopefully, a win. That was as much motivation as I've ever had in my career.

Not only was it motivation, but there was also pride in representing New York after New York had been targeted and devastated. Every American was part of 9/11, but if you lived in the New York area, you lived 9/11. It happened right in our backyard. I had a renewed sense of pride in wearing a gray road jersey with NEW YORK stitched across my chest. And when we resumed play on September 18 and played some road games, there were times we felt like the home team. That's how much support, respect, and sympathy the Yankees received.

Because the 9/11 attacks delayed our schedule by a week, my foot healed enough for me to play in our last few regular season games. I missed fifteen games with that "I must be getting old" foot injury. But it was helpful to get those at bats before the playoffs started against the Oakland A's.

We lost the first two games at the Stadium and we were grasping to keep our season alive. As the designated hitter, I went 0 for 8 and stranded seven runners. Was this the frustrating way my career was going to end? I didn't start Game 3 because left-hander Barry Zito was on the mound for Oakland. That created the possibility of me simply being a spectator in what could have been my final game. Instead, that meant I had a splendid seat to watch Derek Jeter make a miraculous "flip" play in the seventh inning to help preserve our 1-0 win.

With Jeremy Giambi on first, Terrence Long drilled a two-out shot into the right-field corner. As Shane Spencer rushed to retrieve the ball, Giambi rumbled around the bases. When Spencer overthrew two cutoff men, Jeter swooped in from shortstop, grabbed the ball along the first-base line, and then flipped it to Posada. Surprisingly, Giambi didn't slide and Posada tagged him on the leg for the third out, the incredible out. Before Jeter made that phenomenal play, I had never seen a shortstop make it, and I've never seen one make it since.

We showed resilience in that win and it continued as we won the next two games and advanced to the next round. And we exhaled.

Preparing for the ALCS against Lou Piniella's 116-win Mariners, I was reminded of something I had said about Seattle before the playoffs began. I guess I was feeling feisty, because I actually told reporters, "They're a very good team, but you know what? They haven't won anything yet." Well, those words were accurate.

It's one thing to talk the talk. It's another to walk the walk. I would rather walk the walk. I cracked a two-run homer off Aaron Sele to help us to a 4-0 victory in Game 1. And in the deciding Game 5, I had another homer in a 12-3 win as we ended Seattle's splendid season. We had a date with the Arizona Diamondbacks in the World Series, and we were four wins away from bringing some happiness to a lot of wounded Yankee fans.

With Randy Johnson and Curt Schilling as the 1-2 combination in their rotation, the Diamondbacks were a lethal and dangerous team. Suffocating pitching can make a short series feel even shorter. Powerfully and emphatically, Schilling pitched seven one-run innings in the opener and Johnson fired a complete-game three-hitter in Game 2 as the Diamondbacks dominated us. *Gulp*, we were down two games to none.

But we were going home, and the fans, the loyal and still sorrowful fans, were waiting for us. And those games? How can I adequately describe the intensity and that atmosphere? Those were some of the most memorable and spine-tingling games I've ever played in my career, right at the end of it. I will never forget all the American flags being waved in the stands and how many people hugged and celebrated as we tried to give them a wonderful distraction. New York is a huge city, but during those games, it felt like we'd all come together in a small town. There was a camaraderie unlike any other I'd ever experienced between a team and its fans.

We used a very trustworthy formula of Roger Clemens for seven innings and Mariano for two to edge Arizona 2-1 in Game 3 and revive ourselves. That victory was crucial because we would have been in dire straits if we fell behind 3-0 in the best-of-seven series. With one home win, we had a series again.

Then, the ghosts of Yankee Stadium appeared. Down by 2 runs in the ninth inning of Game 4, I singled off Byung-Hyun Kim, the side-arming righty. Kim needed one out to save the game and silence us, but Tino Martinez clubbed a two-run homer to tie the game. The place went berserk. One inning later, as the clock passed midnight and we were participating in the first major-league game to ever be played in November, Derek Jeter poked a walk-off homer to right field against Kim. Unreal. Just unreal. Jeter was baseball's first Mister November.

Before Game 5, one of my brothers, Pat, told a reporter he had started crying in August when he knew my career was ending because I had always been "the youth of the family" and had kept that baseball journey and baseball dream alive. Pat called it a "sad" realization that his little brother wouldn't be playing anymore.

I didn't want to speak to reporters before we played, but this was my final game at the Stadium so I grudgingly agreed to answer some questions. I talked about the Yankees, not me: "If you see a picture representing baseball, you see an old-fashioned baseball with Babe Ruth's autograph and the old bats," I said. "When you walk into this stadium, you feel that because of the history that's been here. Mickey Mantle, Joe DiMaggio. Things haven't changed that much. Those are the things that meant the most to me when I got here, and those are the things that stick with me the whole time I've been here."

The Yankee fans knew I was retiring. Everyone knew. No matter how much I tried to deflect questions about 2001 being my last season, the fans were aware and that's why they turned my final game at Yankee Stadium into one of the most amazing, humbling, and emotional nights of my career.

As I ran pregame sprints across the outfield, the fans chanted my name over and over. When I jogged to my position in right field in the first inning, they gave me a standing ovation. Already? I hadn't done anything. Well, seriously, I knew it was a thank-you for my nine seasons in New York. I lifted my glove to thank them and then I took a couple of deep breaths and gazed around the Stadium to soak up everything that was happening, if that was even possible. I saw posters that read, "Thanks, Paulie."

Standing in the batter's box in the eighth, I was greeted with another standing ovation and my eyes were blitzed by a stream of flashbulbs popping. There were no cell phone cameras back then. The fans were up again for me in the ninth as I stood in right field and I clutched my cap and pulled it over my eyes. I really thought I might cry. That's when the "PAUL O'NEILL, PAUL O'NEILL," chants intensified.

When I heard those chants, I was overwhelmed. I lowered

my head a few times and stared at the outfield grass because I didn't know what to do. We were losing the game, a World Series game! In that setting, it wasn't as if I could wave to the fans or tip my cap or even whisper "Thank you." When you're losing a World Series game, that's not the way you act. I just couldn't do anything. But the fact that the fans cheered while we were losing was quite an honor. It's one of the greatest gifts I've ever received, on or off the baseball field.

And then the game, not me, became the focus as Scott Brosius hit a two-out, game-tying homer off the embattled Kim in the ninth. It was the second straight game in which Kim had surrendered a ninth-inning lead. We were alive again. I batted again in the tenth and grounded out. That was my final at bat at the Stadium because Alfonso Soriano rapped a run-scoring single in the twelfth to lift us to a second straight dramatic win. We led the series, 3-2. No doubt, the fans and the ghosts guided us in the Bronx.

Later that night, I was alone and I tried to process the details from my touching night. I forced myself to embed those memories, every sound and every sight, into my mind so I wouldn't forget what happened. I had always dreamed about fans chanting my name, but in that type of situation? There's no way to plan for receiving adulation while your team is losing a World Series game. That's something that only happens when you're a kid and you're dreaming in your backyard. Actually, let me amend that. It's something that only happens with the devoted Yankee fans at Yankee Stadium. Unbelievable.

The euphoria of New York didn't extend to the games in Arizona. We were walloped 15-2 in Game 6, and Andy Pettitte, who was rocked by the Diamondbacks, later found out he had been tipping his pitches. We had a one-run lead in Game 7 with the ball in Rivera's hand. Three outs to go with Mariano pitching? Ninety-nine times out of a hundred, we would win that game. But this time, we didn't.

Luis Gonzalez's broken-bat, bloop single over a drawn-in infield knocked in the winning run and shocked Mariano, shocked us, and disappointed New York. After the bloop, I walked back to our dugout and lingered. I rested my arms on the railing and watched the Diamondbacks celebrate, a scene I would have found inconceivable fifteen minutes earlier.

In that moment of reflection, I thought about how my career had ended with a loss in the World Series. But in time, here's my recollection of that World Series: the only moments I remember are the three home games because of how gripping they were, how important they were, and how much they meant to the city. Perhaps it's because I retired and I want my final memories to spark some joy, but that's what I will forever cling to from that series.

Did we want to win another World Series? Of course, we did. The outcome was disappointing. But when it was all over and I was packing my gear for the last time, the value of those three games in New York outweighed the final result for me. I'm not sure anyone else shares my opinion, but that's how it felt to me.

And as I reminisce about our run from 1996 to 2001, winning four titles in six seasons was a legendary achievement. There hasn't been a back-to-back champion since we did it more than two decades ago. Looking back on those glorious seasons, I pinch myself every day because I can proudly say I was part of that dynastic period. We had some fantastic people, some excellent players, and some spectacular teams.

Rested and retired in June 2002, I was trying to act like a reporter (and probably failing at it) while working for the YES Network. I was hanging out in the Yankees' clubhouse and talking hitting with Robinson Canó. That's when a serious-looking Torre approached and asked to see me in his office. Oh, no—had I broken a media rule or something? Hardly. It was something much more intriguing than that.

"How long would it take you," Torre asked, "to get ready to play?" I laughed because I thought Joe was joking, but he repeated the same question and added, "We've got some issues we need to address here."

The Yankees were using Shane Spencer, the 1998 super-hero, and John Vander Wal in right field and they weren't satisfied with their production. When Spencer injured his wrist and Torre had to use infielder Enrique Wilson in right, the infielder looked lost. That angered owner George Steinbrenner, who told reporters, "We may make some changes." I guess I was part of that potential change.

My mind went from cruising at 25 miles per hour as I prepared to announce a baseball game to speeding at 90 miles per hour as I tried to process whether I wanted to play in another baseball game. Since my family was leaving for a vacation in Hilton Head Island, South Carolina, the next day, I told Joe I would discuss it with Nevalee and decide if this was something I wanted to consider.

But guess what? I stuffed a couple of baseball gloves in my suitcase and my first day on the beach was spent long-tossing with my son Aaron. Just in case, right? I also ran sprints on the beach, something I hadn't done in over seven months. Just in case, right?

With each hour that passed, I started to think this unexpected comeback might happen and I might get another chance to play baseball. Something that had not even been a faraway thought for me was now a very present thought.

And then I heard from Gene Michael, the Yankees' vice president of major-league scouting, the GM who acquired me from the Reds in 1993. After that gift of a trade, Michael was the first Yankee official I spoke with and the first person who convinced me I could thrive in New York. And now he was supporting this idea, too. "This would be one of the best things that ever happened to you," Michael said. "You've had a mental break and now you can come back. You can still play. You know that and I know that. You can come back and you can do it."

Stick was right. I knew I could have played beyond 2001, but I really wanted my wife and children to have a more stable life and not the all-consuming life of a baseball-player family. Before I retired, I believed I could have played in a reserve role in 2002. But I didn't want to do that. I was always thinking in absolutes: if I wasn't able to play every day anymore, then I wasn't the player I felt I should be.

Still, after Stick's phone call, I took this unofficial offer very seriously. I kept running and throwing. The Yankees had some internal discussions about me possibly going to play for the Triple-A farm team in Columbus, Ohio, which was very close to my home. Could this happen?

The Yankees couldn't wait on me. Several days after my conversation with Joe, the Yankees acquired the power-hitting Raúl Mondesí from the Toronto Blue Jays. The Yankees decided they needed a right fielder immediately and couldn't wait the three or four weeks that it would have taken me to get ready.

I never had a second act and I stayed retired. It's funny, though. I realized how much I missed baseball and how much I still loved baseball, because the possibility of playing again excited me. It scared me, too, but I was poised to hit a few more line drives.

In retrospect, I have always wondered what it would have been like to come back and compete after a layoff. My mind and my body were both so relaxed. The comeback never happened, but I treated the idea seriously. I'm not sure how rusty or smooth my swing would have been, because I never advanced to the point of getting in the batting cage.

Who knows? I could have trained for a few weeks to make this grand return and been billed as a savior of sorts. And knowing me, I probably would have started out 0 for 10 and remembered how maddening it is to be in a slump and said, "The heck with this. I'm going back on vacation."

CHAPTER 10

Extra Innings

The picture still makes me smile, still makes me reminisce, and still makes me feel like a kid again. More than half a century later, I remember posing for the picture in the right-field seats at Crosley Field. Our seats were in the upper deck and seemed pretty close to heaven, which is where the seven-year-old me felt like he was on that momentous day.

I was wearing a red windbreaker, my brown hair was barely peeking out from under my plastic Cincinnati Reds helmet, and I smiled at the camera as if I were about to bat leadoff in NBC's Game of the Week. My elbows were up, my chin was down, and my head was pointed at the pitcher—or, well, the picture-taker, who was my father. By the way, the legendary Roberto Clemente was patrolling right field in the background of the shot.

When my dad asked me to pose for this picture and then asked me to shift about a few inches to my left, he knew exactly what he was doing. Obviously, the O'Neill family wanted to snap a picture of the baby (which was me) at his first major-league game. But my father wanted more than that. He wanted to make sure my everlasting picture included an everlasting player in Clemente.

So smooth, so graceful, and so talented, Clemente was the kind of player you studied on every pitch. Even as a Reds fan, my dad loved to watch Clemente hit, run, and throw because Clemente did everything with a get-out-of-my-way style and a confident approach. Some players are the best on the field for virtually every game of their career. Clemente was one of those giants.

The date of my first game was May 3, 1970. It felt like we were going on a summer vacation, even if that vacation only lasted one day. My mom, my dad, and the six O'Neill kids all piled into the green station wagon with the bench seat and drove 102 miles from our home in Columbus to Cincinnati. I remember our trusty wagon's bench seat because, as the youngest and the smallest, I was always stuck with that uncomfortable spot. But that didn't matter on this day. All that mattered was my heroes were about to come to life.

As I scampered into Crosley for the first time, I was awestruck by everything about the ballpark that had been the Reds' home since 1912. The first thing that jolted me was the sheer size of a major-league field, because I was used to Little League fields. The grass was a vibrant green and was so perfectly mowed, better than any lawn I'd ever seen back in Columbus. The infield was raked so neatly that the dirt looked like a brown blanket. And of course, I smelled the hot dogs, too—a smell that has followed me to every major-league ball-park since then.

Even though the time-worn Crosley was two months away from being replaced by Riverfront Stadium as the Reds' home, it looked like a baseball palace to me. By the time we made it to our seats, I was overwhelmed by everything I had seen. When the players appeared on the field, my backyard dreams burst into life in full color. The game was much more magnificent than anything I could have imagined.

Many years later, I learned that Crosley had been considered one of the coziest ballparks in the majors, because it was only 387 feet to dead-center field and the seating capacity was a mere 29,488. But to a joyous seven-year-old, it was as big a place as I'd ever seen.

I was never the type of kid to keep score of a game, so I remember the power and the speed of those larger-than-life players more than I remember all the statistics from that day. But I do know Johnny Bench cracked a three-run homer and the Reds won 11-7. Pete Rose and Tony Pérez, two men who would later become influential hitting voices for this kid in the plastic Reds helmet, both had two hits. The great Clemente went 1 for 5 with a run scored.

Watching the game intently, I clutched a yellow sheet of paper the way a race-car driver clutches his steering wheel. I couldn't and wouldn't let go. That priceless piece of paper bore an autograph from Clemente! Or did it?

Before the game, I begged my father to help me get Clemente's autograph and told him that would be the greatest gift of my life. My dedicated dad managed to bring me close to a tunnel that led to the visiting team's dugout. It was mobbed with rows and rows of fans and we couldn't get close enough to even ask for an autograph. I cried about our failed attempt, but my dad implored me to enjoy the game and tried to appease me with the picture of me and Clemente.

At some point, my dad left our seats for a while and, miraculously, returned with Clemente's autograph. I couldn't believe what I was now holding in my hands. How did he orchestrate that? Apparently, my father was tired of me whining so he worked some magic and got Roberto Clemente written in blue across that sheet.

My older and wiser brothers waited until we had returned home to spoil my cherished possession by telling me Dad had signed Clemente's name. I refused to believe them and hung tight to the yellow paper. "No way," I told them. "You're just jealous," I added. Eventually, I studied it and realized the signature looked exactly like my dad's.

Oh well...

Interestingly enough, I saw Clemente's last game at Crosley because the Reds relocated to Riverfront starting on June 30, 1970. And even more interestingly, I ended up wearing the same number 21 as the legend I had studied so closely during my first game as a fan. And that was a beautiful accident.

In my first spring training camp with the Reds, the number 57 was hanging in my locker. It's a reliever's number or a linebacker's number, but I didn't say a peep about it. As long as I made it to the majors with the Reds, they could have given me the number 157.

Fortunately, when I debuted with the Reds on September 3, 1985, Bernie Stowe, the kindly clubhouse manager, issued me number 21. I held that jersey in front of me and stared at the back because the 21 jumped out at me. The first thing that dawned on me was how cool that number was because it had been Clemente's number. I didn't wear 21 in high school or in the minor leagues, so it wasn't a number I requested, but as soon as I got it, I never wanted another number.

Every baseball fan should know that the selfless Clemente was as spectacular a humanitarian as he was a player. After an earthquake struck Nicaragua on December 23, 1972, killing more than ten thousand people and leaving up to three hundred thousand homeless, Clemente helped send aid to the country. Clemente tried to fly to Nicaragua on December 31 to make sure the goods were being equitably distributed, but the DC-7 plane, overloaded by more than four thousand pounds of cargo, crashed into the Atlantic Ocean. About one year later, the five-year waiting period was waived and Clemente was enshrined in the Hall of Fame. He was thirty-eight when he died.

In 2021, a fancy box arrived on my doorstep in Ohio, not far from where I'd seen my first game featuring Clemente. When I opened it, I was shocked to find a gorgeous Roberto Clemente watch. The Roberto Clemente Foundation sent me the limited-edition watch honoring Clemente because I had discussed how much I revered him and how much I valued our connection through the number 21 and my first game.

The numbers on the watch are black and gold, matching the uniform colors of Clemente's Pittsburgh Pirates. There is a subtle "21" date marker in gold along the white dial's cir-cumference as an ode to Clemente's number. When I turn the watch over to the back side, there is an image of Clemente. The designers made three thousand watches to match Clemente's career-hit total, and I'm touched to own one of these keepsakes.

—◦◦—

The picture of seven-year-old me at Crosley was made into a baseball card in a series that featured big leaguers when they were kids. It's incredible how the memories flood back when I see that picture. Sometimes, when I'm announcing games for the YES Network, I will peer into the stands, see parents snapping pictures of their children, and wonder if one of them will be the next O'Neill. You never know.

Transitioning from being on the field to being in the broadcast booth was complicated for me. I'm thankful that John J. Filippelli, a Broadcasting Hall of Famer and YES's president of production and programming, had confidence in me and convinced Mr. Steinbrenner to give me a shot behind the microphone. Flip, which is what everyone calls Filippelli, is more of a friend than a boss to me, and he always has timely and intelligent advice. But, in my first year of retirement, I announced some games and it was weird because I felt like I was still playing. I was wearing a suit and tie, but a part of me was still wearing pinstripes, because I believed I could still compete. My heart rate would rise while I was watching my ex-teammates' at bats because I'd put myself in that position and try to think and perform along with them. That made it arduous to separate myself from the dugout mentality and be a totally focused announcer.

These days, I don't have that problem. It's been more than two decades since I played in the majors, and I'm not living every at bat like it's *my* at bat. I no longer think I can still collect hits against sliders and two-seam fastballs. I'm so far removed from my own playing experience that it's much easier for me to watch a game, analyze it, and appreciate how talented these players are.

And if I ever thought I could still have quality at bats in the big leagues, that notion would vanish on Old Timers' Day. That's when I step into the box and just hope I can connect with a 60-mile-per-hour fastball. Believe it or not, that nostalgic day is pretty stressful, because it's the only time all year that I pick up a bat. A few years ago, YES outfitted me with a microphone and an earpiece so I could talk about my at bats as I was playing. After a futile at bat, do you know what I did? I turned off the mic and unplugged the earpiece. I was too frustrated to talk.

Some things never change, I guess.

Other than my early broadcasting adjustment and the Yankees asking me to consider a comeback in the summer of 2002, I made a smooth break from baseball. Once I cut the cord, it was relaxing not to travel for spring training and to be home for Memorial Day, the Fourth of July, and Labor Day— all those holidays I perpetually missed. My bats were placed in storage.

Since many fans hold on to the image of me swinging a bat,

they occasionally ask if I still take batting practice. I sometimes tell them the story about what happened in the batting cage in Cincinnati with my brother Robert and our friends. You know, the time when I wasn't prepared to hit 90-mile-per-hour fastballs and I fouled a ball off a pole and it caromed into a sensitive area of my body? Ouch!

But no, I definitely don't take BP anymore.

A couple of years into retirement, I was amused when an acquaintance tried to recruit me to play in a men's baseball league in Cincinnati. Huh? He sweetened the offer by saying I could pitch. While I had thrown a no-hitter in high school, come on! You've got to be kidding with that idea. I just gave a polite, "No thanks," but I could have said, "You don't go from playing games in Yankee Stadium to playing in an amateur league two years later."

I experienced a much more appealing type of recruiting when I was a junior at Brookhaven High School and Bobby Knight, the legendary basketball coach at Indiana University, contacted me about becoming a Hoosier. If you had asked me then if I was more likely to play baseball or basketball in my future, I probably would have said basketball. While I was in awe of Knight's no-nonsense style and loved our conversation, I later decided to attend the University of South Florida to play baseball for Hall of Famer Robin Roberts and to try to play basketball, too. Once the Reds drafted me, my plans changed.

Anyway, several years ago, I bumped into Knight on the field at Yankee Stadium. We had a pleasant conversation, but I never said anything about his recruitment of me. As the discussion ended, Knight congratulated me on having a stellar baseball career, smiled, and said, "You'd have been a better Hoosier."

Huh? I was shocked. I couldn't believe that Knight, a Hall of Fame coach, remembered recruiting me in the 1980s. I didn't have much of a response, but, as much as I loved playing hoops, Coach Knight was wrong. Baseball was the perfect vocation for me. Hitting was the perfect job for me.

This hitter is retired, but he isn't retired from talking about hitting. I still love to dissect hitters and study hitting. Sometimes, it only takes one sliver of advice to help boost another hitter. Sometimes, I could be the voice that the hitter needs to hear. And remember, hitters will hear a lot of voices with a lot of advice. Be selective.

Working for YES during the 2003 World Series, I watched Jorge Posada taking swings in the batting cage in Miami. I knew Jorge had been fighting himself a bit at the plate, as he had yet to notch any hits against the Marlins. That drought came after he went 8 for 27 (.296 average) with a homer and 6 runs batted in against Boston in the seven-game ALCS.

"What did you try to do," Posada asked, "when you were struggling in big-game situations?"

I told Jorge he needed to keep it simple.

"You've got to try and stay up the middle," I said. "If you don't do that and you start getting big with your swing, you'll start flaring the ball. If you stay up the middle, it gives you an opportunity to pull the breaking ball. And if you're a little late, you can go the other way. And if you're right on it, you can hit a line drive up the middle."

That conversation took about two minutes and I didn't tell

Jorge anything earth-shattering, but it was a way to reassure him and impart some digestible advice. As he returned to the cage, I said, "Line a shot off the BP screen," because that would mean he was hitting the ball up the middle.

A few pitches later, Posada drilled a liner off the screen and I felt as if my advice had made a modest impact. Jorge was one of my all-time favorite teammates because of how tough he was, both physically and mentally. For Jorge to ask me for advice at that delicate point in the season meant as much to me as it did to him. I wasn't playing anymore, but I briefly felt like I was part of the action again. While the Yankees lost that series to the Marlins in six games, Posada had hits in each of the final three games.

I will never stop thinking like a hitter and will willingly offer advice, whether it's to an All-Star like Posada, a minor leaguer, or a neighbor's ten-year-old nephew. I love to discuss the art of hitting, which is why I have compiled seven pieces of advice for young hitters.

BE YOURSELF

The first thing a hitter must be is comfortable, meaning he has to hit in his own way and not in the way his favorite player hits. Don't try to be Mike Trout or Juan Soto. When my sons were playing, they tried to imitate Derek Jeter and Ken Griffey Jr. instead of just hitting comfortably as Aaron O'Neill and Andy O'Neill. There are lessons to be learned by watching how major leaguers hit, but your stance and your approach have to start with you being comfortable and you being you.

HIT LINE DRIVES

My goal was always to hit the ball in the air, just like current hitters who focus on their launch angle. But by hitting the ball in the air, I'm talking about hitting line drives. That's the way my father taught me to hit and that's the way I would advise other fathers to teach their sons to hit. That's what worked for me, and that's still the best approach to me. I tried to hit on top of the ball, stay through the ball and get extension, and hit it hard. As I followed through in my swing, my swing would have a slight uppercut. For me, the perfect swing ended up producing a line drive.

BE A TOUGH GUY (MENTALLY)

Trying to hit a baseball is often a frustrating experience. As Ted Williams said, the toughest thing to do in sports is to hit a round baseball with a round bat. But when a batter experiences some failure, he can't let the exasperation linger and seep into the next at bat. It's difficult to always eliminate negative thoughts and hit with a clean slate, but it will make you a better hitter. I would chant reminders to myself at the plate as a way to accentuate the positive thoughts and diminish the negative thoughts.

HAVE A PLAN

Every hitter needs to have a strategy for what he's trying to do against the pitcher. When Robinson Canó was with the Yankees, I told him the worst thing a hitter could do was change his plan with every pitch. If you do that, you're not being a smart hitter. You're flipping a coin with your approach. When

I executed the timing of my leg kick and put myself in the same position on every pitch, I gave myself the best chance to get a hit. That doesn't mean I resisted making adjustments. If the count advanced to two strikes, I would take a less aggressive swing in trying to drive the ball.

LOOK FOR FASTBALLS

My hitting approach was to look for fastballs that were down the middle or on the outside part of the plate and adjust to every other pitch. I thought that was the best way for me to dictate the at bat and not cater to what the pitcher might do. Some excellent hitters like Posada and Don Mattingly would often guess at what the pitcher might throw, but I was never comfortable doing that. As I said, I even looked for fastballs against Tim Wakefield, a knuckleballer who threw that pitch about 95 percent of the time.

BE A BALANCED BATTER

Every good hitter is a balanced hitter, and every balanced hitter has the leverage and the athleticism to hit the ball to all fields. Being a balanced hitter involves timing. There's a rhythm to it. When a batter strides forward, he wants to be athletic, not rushed, in the lower half of his body because that's where he generates power. If a batter lunges for a pitch and gets out on his front foot too quickly, he's not balanced. With a leg kick, I needed to time it to when the pitcher separated his hand from his glove. If my timing was precise, I would stay balanced and put myself in position to hit the ball squarely.

PRACTICE MAKES PERFECT

This is a no-brainer. If you want to be a great hitter, you must have the drive to get better. You have to work harder than the players in your dugout and definitely harder than the players in the other dugout. I practiced the same way I played: hard. I was always trying to out-hustle someone, whether I was taking swings during the season or working out in the off-season. There were days I felt the need to take 150 swings... before batting practice. The harder I worked, the more I felt I deserved to be successful.

———— ◦⊂⊃◦ ————

There were so many swings, so many at bats, and so many memories, good and bad, throughout my career. I could spend an entire week discussing the at bats I treasured and the at bats I despised. Different at bats resonated with me for different reasons, especially during the stress of the postseason. I remember an at bat against the Mets' Mike Hampton in Game 2 of the 2000 World Series, but one of the reasons I recall it so vividly might seem trite. Here's a hint: it has something to do with a teenage wasteland. Stay tuned. I will explain.

I'm a music fanatic, a drummer, and I've hosted *Name That Tune* parties at my home, so I've always been particular about my walk-up songs. Since the batter hears only a fragment of the song, the music had to slap me in the face quickly. That's why I enjoyed The Who's "Baba O'Riley" as my walk-up song.

I love the beginning of that song, how Pete Townshend

played the electronic organ in a complicated, repetitive pattern, and how this sound stayed embedded in my head. It's one of my all-time favorite songs. If I hear "Baba O'Riley" while shopping in Cincinnati or having dinner in Miami, the first ten seconds take me back to the Bronx.

Before I faced Hampton in the fifth inning, the soundman played "Baba O'Riley" and it gave me an extra jolt. We had a 3-0 lead and two men on base, giving the fans a good reason to be pumped up, too. I had heard a snippet of that song before hundreds of other at bats, but because it was the Subway Series, it sounded a little different and a little more powerful.

On the second pitch of the at bat, Hampton threw an inside fastball and I lined it into the right-field corner for a run-scoring single. I actually clapped my hands running to first base, something I rarely did. And as they played a celebratory song, I wanted to shout, "Hey, D.J., hit me with some more of 'Baba O'Riley.'"

Music fuels my memory of that hit off Hampton. When everyone else reflects on that game, they talk about Roger Clemens whipping a hunk of Mike Piazza's broken bat toward him in the first inning and both benches emptying. That was a tense situation because Clemens had beaned Piazza in the helmet during a game three and a half months earlier. And they will remember Clemens tossing eight shutout innings and striking out nine. And they will recall how we hung on to win 6-5 and take a two-game lead in the series.

I have all of those memories, too. I just have my own musical memory about a song that inspired my RBI single, and that's how "Baba" became part of my hitting routine.

From my position in right field, I could see Monument Park, a hallowed ground located behind the left-center field fence at the old Stadium. That was the place where legends like Babe Ruth, Lou Gehrig, Joe DiMaggio, and Mickey Mantle have been honored with monuments and other Yankee greats have been celebrated with plaques. When it was suggested to me in 1999 that my career could eventually merit a place in Monument Park, I immediately changed the subject.

"It's hard when you're playing to think about that," I said. "I don't really have a quote for that."

And I really didn't have a quote for that hypothetical situation, and I really didn't think about ever receiving such a prestigious honor.

Then the Yankees called me in 2014 and said they wanted to honor me with a plaque in Monument Park.

Wow.

After nine rewarding seasons, four World Series titles, four All-Star berths, one batting title, 1,330 regular season and postseason games, and a thousand cool memories, the Yankees thought I had achieved enough to be placed with their immortals. Okay, now I had to think about a place that seemed so close yet also so far away. I was speechless.

The Yankees have won twenty-seven World Series titles, more than double the amount of any other franchise. The St. Louis Cardinals are second with eleven. There have been fifty-seven Hall of Famers who have played for or worked for the Yankees, another all-time record. You don't need to be a

baseball historian to know the Yankees are the most successful and most storied franchise in baseball history.

And they wanted to put me alongside their legends? I
thought about all of those championships, all of those Hall of
Famers, and all of that history as I processed what it meant to
have a new home in Monument Park.

On a sunny August day, I wore a blue suit and stood on the
infield with my wife, my mother, and my three kids. My five
siblings and other relatives and friends were also at the Stadium. It was a wonderful day, but it was also surreal because
I never wanted to be the focus. However, it was impossible for
me to lurk in the background when it was called "Paul O'Neill
Day." Even the bases had my name printed on the sides.

After my family and former teammates were introduced,
the Yankees asked me to remove the blue-and-white covering
from my monument. Nevalee and I inched over to the plaque,
which was positioned in front of the pitcher's mound, and
lifted off the cover to see my bronzed face. I looked serious
and ready to hit, which was appropriate. Here's what is written
on the plaque:

PAUL ANDREW O'NEILL

"THE WARRIOR"

NEW YORK YANKEES

1993-2001

AN INTENSE COMPETITOR AND TEAM LEADER,

O'NEILL WAS BELOVED FOR HIS RELENTLESS PURSUIT

OF PERFECTION. IN NINE SEASONS WITH THE

YANKEES, HE WON FOUR WORLD SERIES TITLES AND

MADE FOUR ALL-STAR TEAMS, COMPILING A .303
BATTING AVERAGE WITH 185 HOME RUNS AND 855
RBI. WAS ALSO KNOWN FOR HAVING A STRONG ARM
AND RELIABLE GLOVE IN RIGHT FIELD. WON 1994
BATTING CROWN.
DEDICATED BY THE NEW YORK YANKEES
AUGUST 9, 2014

The plaque looked and read perfect, but my head was still spinning from a combination of nerves, anxiety, and excitement. Michael Kay, who is a close friend, a man I trust and the play-by-play announcer whom I've shared a booth with for two decades, invited me to address the fans. Stepping to the microphone, I was more uneasy than if I suddenly had to face Randy Johnson. I spoke for seven minutes and it was just one long thank-you note.

I thanked my mom, my dad, my four brothers, and my sister. I thanked Nevalee and my three kids. I thanked George Steinbrenner and the entire Steinbrenner family. I thanked Yankees executives Brian Cashman, Randy Levine, and Lonn Trost; I thanked Yankees marketing gurus Debbie Tymon and Greg King. I thanked my teammates and, most of all, I thanked the fans. I reminded the fans how special I felt on November 1, 2001, as they repeatedly chanted my name and celebrated me during my final game at the Stadium, Game 5 of the World Series. That's class.

On that day, my plaque was the twenty-ninth the Yankees had placed in Monument Park. Since then, the plaque count has expanded to thirty-eight, as my teammates Derek Jeter,

Mariano Rivera, Jorge Posada, Bernie Williams, Andy Pettitte, Manager Joe Torre, and coaches Willie Randolph and Mel Stottlemyre have received plaques as well. There are also seven monuments in this prestigious spot, including one for Mr. Steinbrenner, the Boss.

In the "new" Yankee Stadium, Monument Park is housed behind center field. It's an unbelievable honor and it's endlessly humbling to know that I am recognized there. I never pondered that possibility until it became a reality, and man, I'm so proud that it happened. As I said through a cracked voice that day, my dad was smiling about the honor.

The plaque in Monument Park was an amazing honor and was an incredible celebration of my career. This kid from Columbus, Ohio, somehow had a place next to the greatest players in Yankees' history. I was truly humbled and truly content. But, on a sunny morning in February of 2022, I learned my place in that illustrious history was going to be elevated even more. Debbie Tymon, the Yankees' tireless and brilliant senior vice president of marketing, called me, and, after we talked for a few minutes, she told me she had some news to share.

"Paul," she said, "I wanted to let you know the Yankees are going to retire your number 21 this season."

I was shell-shocked. I dropped the phone and stumbled through some version of "Thank you." I wasn't expecting this, and I wasn't prepared for it. I whispered it to Nevalee, and she began crying. Do you know how people say something gives them goose bumps? We hear that expression, and we understand it, but do we believe that person actually had goose bumps on their arms? Well, I did. Both arms. For a long time. I was trying to grasp the magnitude of this reward.

"This," I finally told my family and friends, "is my Hall of Fame."

After Debbie broke the news about my number being retired on August 21, 2022, Hal Steinbrenner, the Yankees' managing general partner, called to congratulate me. Hal was gracious and complimentary about my career and explained why number 21 should be retired. He also told me how I had been one of his father's favorite players, and, of course, I know some of Mr. Steinbrenner's affinity for me had to do with my fiery approach to the game. Mr. Steinbrenner was a hands-on owner who had an unbelievable passion for winning, and I tried to match that passion with the way I played.

I'm thankful to Mr. Steinbrenner, Hal, and the entire Steinbrenner family for the support and loyalty they have shown me and my family during my time as a player and a broadcaster in New York, a career that now includes the number 21 on my back being immortalized.

I could speak about the organization's kindness and generosity for days and still not say enough. But thank you for helping my dreams come true.

If someone is accomplished enough to have his number retired by a high school or a college, that's impressive. When it happens at the professional level, it's even more impressive. But when I thought about the fact that my number 21 was being retired by the Yankees, the most successful and recognizable baseball team of all time, I shook my head and reflected about how rare and phenomenal that was.

The first retired numbers I thought about were those worn by the immortals like Babe Ruth (number 3), Lou Gehrig (4), and Joe DiMaggio (5), but then I remembered how I had the opportunity to meet the legendary Mickey Mantle (7), have conversations with the great Whitey Ford (16), and become friends with the one-of-a-kind Yogi Berra (8). And then my mind raced to Roger Maris (9), Phil Rizzuto (10), Thurman Munson (15), Elston Howard (32), Reggie Jackson (44), and several others.

It's mind-blowing to think I'm mixed in with those players. In the most honest and realistic way, I told my family, "I'm coming off the bench on this team. There's no way I'm in the starting lineup." And you know what? That's the most extraordinary team I could ever imagine. I'm so humbled to be in that grouping with twenty-two other Yankee players and managers.

And, as I look at those retired numbers magnificently painted on the blue wall behind the left-center field seats at Yankee Stadium, I'm beyond proud to be in the same neighborhood with many of my contemporaries and friends. I have such fond memories of playing with Don Mattingly (23), Derek Jeter (2), Mariano Rivera (42), Andy Pettitte (46), Bernie Williams (51), and Jorge Posada (20) and, of course, of being managed by the great Joe Torre (6). To know that my number will forever be side by side with theirs just further cements the bond that we already have. Aside from Donnie, the rest of us were involved in winning four championships in five years, so a lot of great things happened in a short period of time. And the retired numbers are the individual rewards for performing on those superb teams. It's the greatest honor a player could receive.

Eternity. When your number is retired, it's retired forever.

When I thought about my place in this special Yankees' club, I discussed it with Nevalee and my three kids. And, as we spoke through happy tears, the honor began to resonate even more.

"No Yankee will ever number 21 again," they all said to me. "Think about that. Think about how huge an honor that is."

After it was framed in that meaningful way, it was a reminder that my retired number 21 will be something powerful I can pass on to my family's future generations. My grandkids and my great-grandkids will look at that number 21 on the blue wall at the Stadium someday, and they will be told what I did to make it happen. And that's a legacy that gives me goose bumps all over again.

In the dizzying period after I learned my number would be retired, I woke up every morning and asked myself, "Did this really happen or am I dreaming?" I keep thinking about how cool this is, how everlasting this is, and how I can't supply enough superlatives to describe how I feel about it.

Since my retirement, the only Yankee to wear number 21 during the regular season was LaTroy Hawkins, who wore it briefly in 2008. LaTroy wanted to wear it to honor Roberto Clemente, which I respect and understand. But some fans protested, and it became a distraction for LaTroy, and he switched to number 22. Anyway, even though the number 21 has essentially been out of circulation on the Yankees, I didn't spend a lot of time wondering about the possible retirement of the number. The Yankees have always recognized my contributions and treated me with respect, so I never questioned their decisions.

And then they made a decision to give me the ultimate

honor. Wow. That word only contains three letters, but that word says it all.

Every time I visit Yankee Stadium, no Yankee will be wearing the number 21, because it will be hanging there, not too far from the mighty Babe or the tenacious Thurman or the smooth Jeter or the invincible Mariano. I've always smiled when I see fans still wearing my number 21 at games, because that means they are diehards who appreciated what I once did.

Well, I guess I will have a perpetual smile at the Stadium because I'm going to stare at that 21 every time I'm there now.

Like I said, *Wow.*

My baseball odyssey started very early. I was swinging a bat when I was two years old, and I was chasing my four older brothers around the backyard and around local baseball fields soon after that. And when I was six years old, my father actually told me, "Paul, you're going to play in the big leagues one day."

Yes, my dad really uttered those prophetic words. I guess the man I called Little Buddy and Old-Timer was that confident in his son's swing. As powerful as that statement was, I figured every father said that to every son, so I just kept swinging away. But my dad insisted he was serious about his prediction, and because of the support from him, my mom, my siblings, and my wife, he ended up being right.

It has been a glorious journey for me, a life filled with baseball, family, and more baseball, and a life in which I was able to achieve the dreams I had as a kid. I feel beyond fortunate and beyond blessed that I lived mine. My recipe for success was hard work, persistence, stubbornness, and line drives—always line drives. It took a lot of swings and a lot of hits.

ACKNOWLEDGMENTS

———◁▷———

I have always loved hitting. Ever since I played baseball in the backyard with my older brothers, hitting has been an obsession. Once I retired from the Yankees in 2001, I've still loved talking about hitting on the YES Network and with current and former players. Since I'm not hitting in the major leagues anymore, talking about it is the next best thing.

When Jack Curry presented me with the idea of turning my thoughts, lessons, and anecdotes about hitting and hitters into a book, I was very intrigued. While I would never force my opinions on anyone, this book was a wonderful way to share everything I've learned along my baseball journey with interested fans and readers.

I actually told Jack he's the only person who I would have collaborated with on this book because I respect him and I trust him. I've known Jack since I first joined the Yankees for the 1993 season, and we're now colleagues at YES. He is skilled at asking pertinent questions and then framing my thoughts perfectly. I'm so glad we partnered on this book.

Like anything else in my life, this book wouldn't have been

Acknowledgments

completed without the help of Nevalee, my wife of thirty-eight years. I've often joked that Nevalee is my eyes and my ears, but it's really not a joke. She always makes sure that I'm in the right place at the right time. Thanks for everything, Mama. I also must thank my three kids, Andy, Aaron, and Allie, and their spouses and my grandchildren, who are truly the home runs of my life.

Speaking of family, I'm honored to have been a part of the Yankee family for almost three decades. George Steinbrenner always treated me with great respect, and I'm forever grateful for what he did for my family. From day one in pinstripes until now, the Steinbrenners have always made me feel a part of the great Yankees' family. We can't thank them enough. Along with the Steinbrenners, I would also like to thank Brian Cashman, Randy Levine, Lonn Trust, Debbie Tymon, and Greg King of the Yankees for their support. In addition, I'm appreciative of the former teammates who helped with this book. And I have to thank all of the Cincinnati Reds' and New York Yankees' fans who have always been so kind to me.

I also have a TV family at YES, headed by John J. Filippelli, my boss and the man who Mr. Steinbrenner hired to create YES. Flip is a great friend and someone I could talk baseball with for hours. The YES lineup is filled with talented friends and colleagues, especially my booth buddies, Michael Kay and David Cone.

Finally, I'm happy to have become teammates with Sean Desmond and David Black on this project. From our first meeting, I could tell how professional they were and how much they cared about making this book a success. I'm proud of what we've produced. I hope you enjoy it.

—Paul O'Neill

I've talked about hitting with Paul O'Neill for close to thirty years. There have been captivating interviews, riveting conversations, and informative chats. After absorbing O'Neill's passion and insight for so long, I finally asked him if he wanted to collaborate on a book. He liked the concept, and our partnership produced *Swing and a Hit*.

"I'm doing this book," Paul said, "because I trust you."

That trust was an important factor and worked both ways: Paul trusted me to accurately tell his story, and I trusted him to share the most interesting aspects of his life and career. And he did. Paul's philosophies about hitting are compelling, and his recollections of his teammates, opponents, and managers are also fascinating. I'm proud to have transferred Paul's thoughts into the words in this book.

Along this writing journey, I'm thankful to have been supported by Sean Desmond, an elite editor, and the rest of his talented team. I'm also grateful for the wisdom of David Black, my literary agent and my ally. Like O'Neill, both men are all-stars in their fields and made this process run smoothly.

While working on this book, I appreciated the steadfast support of John J. Filippelli, my boss at the YES Network and my friend, too. His passion for baseball and for great stories, like the ones O'Neill shared, is unmatched. I'm fortunate to have so many YES colleagues who are my friends and who listened to me discuss the book or made suggestions, including Jared Boshnack, Michael Kay, Bob Lorenz, John Flaherty, David Cone, Meredith Marakovits, Nancy Newman, Kevin Sullivan, Troy Benjamin, Josh Isaac, and Mike Medvin. Brielle Saracini and Heather Smith were my friends long before they were my colleagues. Researchers Jeff Quagliata and James Smyth were thorough and fast with information.

Ian O'Connor, Joel Sherman, Mike Vaccaro, and Don Burke are close friends and excellent journalists who provided advice. Greg Gutes, a savvy editor, was kind enough to review these pages. I'm lucky to have a family filled with supporters, including my brother, Rob, my sisters-in-law, Suzanne and Tracey, my nephews, Ian, Kyle, and Shane, and my baseball-obsessed father-in-law, Mr. O. Now that this book is finished, I'm waiting for Dylan Acree to interview me for his movie and for A. J. Castro to write his book report.

Besides asking Paul dozens of questions, I also interviewed his former managers, teammates, and opponents. I thank them for their time. Nevalee, Paul's wife, was invaluable in helping with this project.

Of course, I saved the best for last. No one spoke with me about this book as much as Pamela, my sweet and selfless wife. She is my best friend and my soul mate, but she's also a part-time adviser, a part-time editor, and a full-time cheerleader. Thank you, Bean.

Because of the countless hours required, the completion of

a book is always a reason to celebrate. After I wrote the final words, my celebration involved listening to some Bob Marley. The words that resonated with me were "Don't worry about a thing 'cause every little thing gonna be all right."

—Jack Curry

INDEX

Index

Index

Index

Index

Index

Index

ABOUT THE AUTHORS

PAUL ANDREW O'NEILL played seventeen seasons in the major leagues. He played for the Cincinnati Reds (1985–1992) and New York Yankees (1993–2001). O'Neill compiled 281 home runs, 1,269 runs batted in, 2,107 hits, and a lifetime batting average of .288. He won the American League batting title in 1994 with a .359 average. He was a five-time World Series champion and a five-time All-Star (1991, 1994, 1995, 1997, and 1998). After retiring from playing baseball, O'Neill became a broadcaster for the Yankees on the YES Network. He currently works on the network as the lead game analyst and color commentator.

JACK CURRY is an award-winning sports journalist who is an analyst on the Yankees' pregame and postgame shows on the YES Network, where he has worked since 2010. He has won five New York Emmy Awards. Before joining YES, he covered baseball for twenty seasons at *The New York Times*, first as a Yankee beat writer and then as a national baseball correspondent. Curry is also the coauthor of two *New York Times* bestsellers: *Full Count: The Education of a Pitcher*, with David Cone and *The Life You Imagine* with Derek Jeter. He currently lives in New Jersey.